The Spiritual Genius of
Saint Thérèse of Lisieux

The Author

Jean Guitton was born in 1901. He taught philosophy in Troyes, Moulins, Lyon, and Montpellier in the 1930s, and was a prisoner of war from 1940 to 1945. In 1955 he was appointed Professor of Philosophy at the Sorbonne and was elected to the French Academy in 1961. He was the only layperson authorized by Pope John XXIII to attend the first session of the Second Vatican Council in 1962. The latest of his many books are a series of interviews on the subjects of God, faith, and the future: *Chaque jour que Dieu fait* (Each Day God Makes; 1995), *Une recherche de Dieu* (A quest for God; 1996), *Le siècle qui s'annonce* (The Coming Century; 1997).

The Translator

Felicity Leng was educated at St Mary's Convent, Ascot, England, and the Slade School of Fine Art, University College, London. She has taught art and languages in Britain and in France, where she has lived for many years. She is a professional painter and photographer, as well as a translator, and her work in both media has been exhibited in Paris, Edinburgh, and elsewhere in Scotland. St Thérèse has been a lifelong interest of hers, and she is currently working on a study of the saint in relation to other women of her time.

D1489115

THE SPIRITUAL GENIUS
OF
SAINT THÉRÈSE OF LISIEUX

Jean Guitton

Translated by
FELICITY LENG

LIGUORI/TRIUMPH
LIGUORI, MISSOURI

Published by Liguori/Triumph
An Imprint of Liguori Publications
Liguori, Missouri

First published in Great Britain in 1997
by Burns & Oates
Wellwood, North Farm Road
Tunbridge Wells, Kent TN2 3DR

Original edition *Le Génie de Thérèse*
Published by Editions de l'Emmanuel, Paris
Copyright © Editions de l'Emmanuel, March 1995

English translation © Copyright Burns & Oates, 1997

Library of Congress Cataloging-in-Publication Data

Guitton, Jean
    [Génie de Thérèse de Lisieux]
    The spiritual genius of Saint Thérèse of Lisieux / Jean Guitton : translated by Felicity Leng. — 1st ed.
       p. cm.
    Includes bibliography, index.
    ISBN 0-7648-0077-9 (alk. paper)
    1. Thérèse, de Lisieux, Saint, 1873-1897. I. Title.
BX4700. T5G83 1997
282'.092—dc21
  [B]   97-1640

01 00 99 98   5 4 3 2

Printed in the United States
Typeset by Search Press Ltd

Contents

Abbreviations

All references, unless otherwise indicated, are to the orignal French manuscripts or authorized published editions of Thérèse's and associated works.

A   Manuscript A (1895)

B   Manuscript B (1896)

C   Manuscript C (1897)
           by St Thérèse, with an indication whether the page
           is recto (r) or verso (v).

CSG   *Conseils et Souvenirs* (Advice and Memories)
           by Sr Geneviève (Céline Martin)

DE   *Derniers Entretiens* (Last Discourses)

LT   *Lettres*
           Letters of St Thérèse, numbered as in the French
           edition

PN   *Poésies*
           Poems of St Thérèse, numbered as in the French
           edition.

References to the Complete Works are to *Oeuvres complètes de sainte Thérèse*, published in one volume (Paris, 1992).

Translator's Note

I have expanded a number of M. Guitton's references which would require a knowledge of French and world literature and so on which English-language readers cannot be assumed to possess. I have also added a chronology of Thérèse's life and of subsequent relevant events which enables occasions and works referred to by M. Guitton to be located appropriately.

Felicity Leng

Foreword

by Mgr Guy GAUCHER
Auxiliary Bishop of Bayeux-Lisieux

In 1954, Jean Guitton had written an *"Essay on the Spiritual Genius in the Teaching of St Thérèse of the Child Jesus,"* published by the *Annales of Lisieux.* This text was amplified in 1965 in a booklet with various articles added, under the title *Le Génie de sainte Thérèse de l'Enfant-Jésus.*

I, personally, found reading these pages a deeply touching experience since, at the time, it was rare for a philosopher to be interested in the person intellectuals tended to consider as "a nice little saint with roses." Of course, some leading thinkers, such as Bergson, and very many theologians, had plumbed the deep simplicity of the saint from Lisieux. But, dazzled by the statement by the Russian Orthodox Merezhkovsky which placed Thérèse on the heights of religious thought with Saints Paul, Augustine, Francis of Assisi, and Joan of Arc, Jean Guitton wrote some pages which shed a new light on Thérèse's thought.

By analyzing seven of her "key words," he showed what depth—or what height—Thérèse's intuition could reach when one knows how to read her.

Reading Guitton made such an impression on me that it made me regret more than ever that he never wrote the book on Thérèse that we might have hoped for, as he had done on Joan of Arc.

As we celebrate the centenary of the *dies natalis* (birthday in heaven, i.e., death) of the Carmelite (1997), it is the right moment to re-issue Guitton's thoughts on Thérèse, which have long been unavailable. We are all very grateful to Jean Guitton for authorizing us to re-issue his thoughts for a wide public in a form finally worthy of their content. They will add to the voices of all those throughout the world who are asking Pope John Paul II to proclaim St Thérèse of the Child Jesus and the Holy Face a Doctor of the Church. May the philosopher, the theologian, and the People of God together be heard at the dawn of the third millennium, as the wonders worked by God through Thérèse—that spiritual genius—are still to come.

Preface

On re-reading what I wrote about Thérèse forty years ago, I find that I wish to make no changes to the original text. I have always tried to write in as timeless a manner as possible, believing that what is true for today is also true for tomorrow and forever.

One of my mentors once said, "You should write in such a way as to provide food for the mind and nourishment for the soul," and I have always tried to follow this advice. Accordingly, I should like to think that what I have written is still entirely relevant.

Three saints, Thérèse, Elizabeth, and Edith, were constantly in my mind as I wrote and, in a very real sense, are present throughout this book. I was deeply attracted and intrigued by their distinctiveness yet underlying similarity. Since my method is essentially comparative, I was constantly comparing them even when I did not mention them explicitly.

Thérèse's autobiography has been one of the best-sellers of the twentieth century. It has sold millions of copies and has been translated into more than forty languages. Why is that? Because Thérèse, in simple, childlike, and unsophisticated yet uniquely inspired language touched by genius, is able to tell us what all the mystics have always said: love, not the this or that of love, is everything; and a single act of love, silent, pure, and simple, is worth more than all ascetic practices. This absolute primacy of love is expressed in the phrase *Deus caritas est*—"God is love."

Certain traits in the character of Thérèse of the Child Jesus, especially her mixture of spontaneity and apparent naiveté, were once thought of as typically feminine, yet they were interfused with an assurance and determination both compelling and exacting that helped to make her the unusual person she was in her particular time and place. A woman must be either a sinner or a saint, in the natural or in the supernatural order. There is no such thing as a woman who is just a woman; and Thérèse was no exception.

I dedicated the first edition of this book to Mgr Montini, Archbishop of Milan (later Pope Paul VI). He was baptized on the day Thérèse died, which still seems worthy of record, though, of course, the dedication itself is no longer relevant. Instead I now offer the following lines:

> Dearest, gentlest, purest, fairest,
> Loveliest, meekest, blithest, kindest,
> Lead, we seek the home thou findest.
>
> *(John Henry Newman, in memory of his*
> *sister Mary, aged seventeen)*

I think that Newman's verses on his sister Mary's death in her eighteenth year are an admirable description of Thérèse. Since 1910, like the image of a sister struck dead in the flower of her youth, her ethos and principles may be thought of as standing for the spiritual guidance that has helped modern humanity to emerge from two terrible world wars. Not only that. For so many human beings, then, now, and on other occasions, Thérèse has actually been their Sister and Angel in harsh times. Above all, for a vast company of people, she has been the angelic guide who reveals the simple way to do what is most difficult: which is to love. This, of course, is the message of all the mystics, and in particular that of the mysterious author of *The Imitation of Christ*. Thérèse used this book in her prayer life, distilled its essence, and passed it on to us in her own unique way. For my own part, I have always felt that *The Trial of Joan of Arc*, *The Imitation of Christ*, and *The Story of a Soul* are three intimately-related gospels, with something very special to say to those who are sensitive to their individual and joint resonance.

Jean Guitton
Rome, October 1, 1994

Introduction

Many artists have tried to reproduce the scene of the boy Jesus sitting in the temple among the teachers and learned men, "both hearing them, and asking them questions," that Luke describes at the beginning of his Gospel. "And all that heard him were astonished at his understanding and answers." The occasion has a timeless appeal, because in every period the old and the young are drawn to one another. Knowledge overwhelmed by knowing too much, even knowledge at the end of its tether, is or may be captivated and revivified by knowledge of a different order—by the intuitive wisdom of those with little or no learning.

I think of the adolescent Jesus as calm, intent, attentive and with a clear gaze—with "eyes so simple, so pure, so clear" (as St Catherine of Genoa noted when she thought of angels)—encircled by a crown of scholars' heads heavy with profundity. They hold the scroll of the Scriptures firmly, for they are masters of its word, yet it is silent in their hands. The text of the Law is their law and guidance, yet they cannot agree on the one true meaning of the text, and interpretations abound. The German poet and dramatist Schiller said: "When kings build, wheelbarrows have a lot of work." The child among the scholars may be God and child, but he is not an infant prodigy. Luke does not tell us that he is teaching the elders. He listens to them and he asks them questions, just as he does later on the road to Emmaus, after his death, at the end of Luke's Gospel: "What is this conversation which you are holding with each other as you walk?" "Why are you troubled and why do questions arise in your hearts?" Jesus always liked posing awkward questions, even to his mother and the apostles. The sober-faced elders were most intrigued by the assurance of such a young person. It is all very reminiscent of the behaviour of the young Pascal, whose similarly clear yet inquiring mind brought tears of joy to his father Étienne's eyes. There have been many such occasions in the past, though there is reason to think that the number will gradually diminish, even though our civilization, now so very old and overwhelmed by uncertainty and insecurity, is in greater need than ever of young people who can ask the right questions in the right way. In the future, one suspects, the development of the precocious Pascal and similar children throughout history will become all but impossible because mathematics, both higher and applied, has become incredibly complex and ramified. Moreover, the necessary technology and associated facilities are not only beyond the grasp of any child but, on the scale now paradoxically required to prompt and exercise even this particular kind of early acute simplicity and intuitive rather than mechanical brilliance, will eventually exceed the financial and therefore educational resources of almost every modern nation.

Nor will that particular kind of nurture be possible in the fields of philosophy or theology, let alone in the art of military tactics and strategy, as it was in the time of Joan of Arc. But what about poetry? Here again there are so many cases in which child poets are merely stretching cleverness over inexperience, or just imitating the transiently fashionable childishness of their elders. Wherever we look, there is scarcely any area other than the spiritual life where this particular kind of childlike wisdom is likely to be found. There the synthetic approach pure and simple is still the ideal. There alone, though in very rare cases, a young person with an exceptionally limpid mind, if brought up appropriately, could—so to speak from the outset—achieve the simplicity revealed to wise men and scholars only after much effort, many setbacks, and long-drawn-out but patient speculation. In this sense, surely, Jesus suggested that those who wanted to follow him should be as little children, and voluntarily rediscover what a child could be, not as a reward for great industry, but naturally and intuitively. As Thérèse wrote (at the end of her first manuscript dedicated to Mother Agnes of Jesus) of an occasion during the period before she entered Carmel: "Jesus came down to my level, and taught me the lesson of love quite secretly. If learned men who had spent their lives studying had come to question me, they would surely have been astonished to find a fourteen-year-old girl who understood the secrets of perfection, secrets which all their expert knowledge wouldn't help them to find, since only the poor in spirit can possess them."

* * *

When I look critically at the personality and work of, and the counsel offered by, Thérèse of the Child Jesus, all my queries, investigations, and study lead to one central question.

No one, least of all in Catholic circles, could deny that Thérèse should be considered a religious saint, a saintly religious, worthy of canonization as well as canonized, and an immensely attractive personality: one with, in other words, not only a halo but an aura of what can only be called charm or, to use the vogue word, charisma. But the question is not really whether Thérèse belongs to the general communion of saints but whether she should be ranked among the much smaller company of saints of that rare and special degree of insight that can only be called genius. Is she to be counted among those very exceptional people who have drawn on the perennial storehouse of evangelical truth to offer us quite novel ways and, indeed, truths of life? I must admit that for many years this particular question never occurred to me (being merely interested in, though not emotionally captivated by, Thérèse of the Child Jesus). But I was imprisoned during the war. Then I happened to read, and had time to meditate on, a book with the curious title *From Jesus to Us*, by Dmitri Merezhkovsky (1865-1941), a Russian Orthodox philosopher, thinker, poet, novelist, and critic.

Merezhkovsky is a fascinating and unjustly forgotten figure. He was born in St Petersburg and was very influenced by Dostoievsky, whom he knew personally, and a host of other writers and thinkers from Comte to Baudelaire. He was a pioneer of the "symbolist" and "modernist" movements and wrote philosophical novels. He took refuge in Paris in 1920, after the Russian Revolution, and produced biographies of Calvin, Luther, Napoleon, and Dante. He was married to the sensitive Russian symbolist poet Zinaida Hippius. Almost everything he wrote was opposed to crass materialism and stressed the mysterious higher reality of another, superior world, though some of his most interesting writing comes from an attempt to show that such a conviction demands not a denial of physicality but its reconciliation with spirituality. He wrote a historical trilogy, *Christ and the Antichrist*, but it is *From Jesus to Us* that is most relevant to our theme.

Merezhkovsky's subtle Slav mind proceeds in leaps and bounds and sudden bursts of insight. Apart from eliciting the virtues of Pascal, Calvin, and Napoleon, he suggests that, from Jesus to our time, there have been only five or six saints of genius who have, so to speak, passed on the torch of enlightenment in this world: the first four on his list are St Paul, St Augustine, St Francis of Assisi, and St Joan of Arc. I was intrigued to find him tackling this particular issue, as I had asked myself essentially the same question when trying to work out who, in different areas of achievement, were the most important saints (much as one does with, say, philosophers, the really original thinkers whom, since Plato, you can count on your fingers). I had arrived at almost the same set of names. After St Joan of Arc and St Teresa of Avila, I had hesitated, confused by the host of possibilities in modern times pressing their claims on my judgment for this or that good reason. This is understandable, for remoteness eradicates the merely worthy but familiarity in time can breed too much respect.

Merezhkovsky did not hesitate. Being a Russian and a non-Catholic, with absolute assurance he named Thérèse of the Child Jesus as an obvious member of this select company. He compared her with Joan of Arc, discerning the same spirit in both of them, though Thérèse extended it to accommodate the dimensions, difficulties, and terrible and imminent conflicts of the modern world. All very well, but why exactly was that possible? Because, he said, Joan and Thérèse had extraordinarily innovative minds and attitudes. Instead of looking at saintliness as a way of climbing toward a heaven outside this world, they believed that heaven had to be seen as carrying on, as an extension of, our real mission: the work we have been given to do on earth. Like God its creator, they really loved the human world not as a means to an end but for its own sake. Those famous words were actually very revolutionary: "I want to spend my time in heaven doing good on earth."

We might also say that Thérèse rediscovered the positive aspects of Luther's intuitive understanding of what was most important, as in her self-surrender to merciful love (something like "the act of self-abandonment" described in the works of the two French spiritual writers Claude de La Colombière and Auguste Valensin). Here Thérèse certainly hit upon the powerful and lasting point of what Luther said about the saving power of faith over and beyond good works. It is also far from straining comparisons to detect in her "nothing unless for today," in her notion that the whole of eternity is already present in each exquisite fleeting moment, the same truth that in 1897, the year of Thérèse's death, the French novelist André Gide (born and raised a Protestant) presented, though in an "inverted," pantheistic, and aesthetic form, in his famous *Nourritures terrestres* (Earthly Pastures). Gide's book concentrates on the importance not of "glorifying desire and the instincts" but of personal effort in the sense of total self-giving, lived experience, joyous appreciation of the body and nature, spontaneity and sensuous generosity,

and there is something very similar in Thérèse. More generally, we might say that that love of the world of common
humanity, of the humble, militant, and suffering human
condition, of "little people" of "limited means" and of the
despised of the earth, of simple, passing, insignificant and
forgotten actions, of constant sincerity, of commitment, of
the place of all small and genuine people and impulses in the
totality of things—in short, of all that is best in what I do not
scruple to call the immanent spirituality of the modern
world—is already to be found, whole and entire, in Thérèse
of the Little Child Jesus. Not only the foregoing but even
darker aspects of the modern awareness were present in her,
right up to and including existential anguish, the experience
of radical doubt about everything whatsoever, and a quasi-
Baudelairean sense of the void, of ultimate nothingness. It
may seem strange to think of little Thérèse in this respect, but
she certainly experienced all this, as a death harsher than
death itself, during the last years of her life.

Although some people might think that I have overstated
the case in what I have to say about the insights and sensibility
of genius in Thérèse, in fact, paradoxical though this may
seem, the message of sheer simplicity is an all but inexhaustible source of matter for profitable comment and explanation.
After all, there are two types of simplicity, just as there are two
types of childhood: the simplicity of having nothing at all, the
childhood of being born and starting off in life, which is only
an image of the ultimate objective; and the simplicity of
completion and true achievement: the childhood which it is
actually impossible to "achieve," and which is a kind of return
of the mature human being to his or her one true source.

The chapters that follow are an attempt to shed new light
on the message of St Thérèse, and to show how, far from
being a merely likeable if quaint little figure with a mentality
wholly explicable in terms of, and inseparable from, the more
provincial aspects of her country and Church in the late

nineteenth century, she is profoundly relevant now. Her message, offered in and through what she was and what was to hand, connects with some of the most vital spiritual currents of our own time.

HER CHARM

What does the special charm of any human being consist in? It is difficult to say, because the idea of charm is indefinable. It is a certain presence of a person that is immaterial, something that extends beyond his or her bounds, so to speak. It is like the radiance that emanates from some simply quite perfect faces. It is also a certain ease of gesture, words, behaviour and even the most seemingly insignificant actions and movements, which nevertheless makes this or that person seem a gesture from another dimension made in our own, to which the individual in question responds fluently and effortlessly, as he or she communicates naturally with the source of all that is simply good and right. A person who charms you smoothes away your tensions, wrinkles of concern, self-doubts, fears of danger, fear of others and, most important of all perhaps, fear of yourself. You are relaxed, relieved of an inner burden, and left free but also prepared to hear and respond to the message of a higher reality: that summons from God which should possess what we call "charm" to the highest possible degree. Certainly God cannot be perceived, even for an instant, unless you get entirely, even leap, outside yourself, and are quite drawn away from all mundane things into the sheer beauty of his Beauty. The practitioners of divine justice forget at their peril the divine charm which attracts and irradiates all souls even touched by glory.

Only a few saints have charm like this, in the sense of real charisma. Perfect charm does not wholly accord with adults. I would not say that St Francis of Assisi or St Francis de Sales possessed in the full sense the attribute which I am trying to define, which needs a special kind of childlike nature. Although children may appear charming, they do not have real charm, which implies asceticism, self-detachment, and a total lack of awareness that one has it. Being conscious of having charm would be like actors being aware of their role, in which case it would be a transient charm, which is a very different thing.

Charm and approach or attitude are almost one and the same thing in Thérèse. What Newman said of St John Chrysostom, to whom we may be said to owe the whole concept of straightforward or literal exegesis, could also apply to her: "It is not force of words, nor cogency of argument, nor harmony of composition, nor depth nor richness of thought, which constitutes his power,—whence, then, has he this influence, so mysterious, yet so strong? I consider St Chrysostom's charm to lie in his intimate sympathy and compassionateness for the whole world, not only in its strength, but in its weakness; in the lively regard with which he views everything that comes before him . . . It was not by the fertility of his imagination, or the splendour of his diction that he gained the surname of 'Mouth of God.' . . . His unrivalled charm, as that of every eloquent man, lies in his singleness of purpose, his fixed grasp of his aim, his noble earnestness . . . I speak of the discriminating affectionateness with which he accepts everyone for what is personal in him and unlike others . . . I speak of the kindly spirit and the genial temper with which he looks round at all things which this wonderful world contains" (*Historical Sketches*, vol. II, p. 234). Moreover, Newman remarks, there are many commentators on Scripture who adhere to the letter, but there is only one John Chrysostom, and it is Chrysostom who is the "charm of the method, not the method that is the charm of Chrysostom." I do not know that this distinction between charm and method really applies to Chrysostom (known as "Golden Mouth") exactly as Newman so neatly puts it. But the word "charm," if ever it could be applied to a saint, perfectly characterizes and even defines Sr Thérèse of the Child Jesus. Her charm took her ahead at an unusual pace and made her stand out at an early age. It has made her so universally loved that she has pushed more conventionally distinguished saints into the background. That is why it is so difficult to separate her method from her personality, and why, in this sense, her approach is not so transparent as it seems to be and as Thérèse obviously thought it was.

In what follows, I am going to venture off well-beaten tracks in an attempt to define some aspects of Thérèse's method and teaching. I shall examine these aspects under the headings of seven key terms taken from Thérèse's writings, which open up seven paths, old and new, to the spiritual life.

I could have chosen others, to be sure, and I do not claim to have made a perfect choice or that someone else would necessarily make the same selection. But I do think that those topics chosen under the perennially if mysteriously effective seven heads cover the main aspects of Thérèse's character. For the most part I have avoided any reference to well-worn quotations from Thérèse's works. For example, I have ignored those in which "childhood" occurs because, especially in the present context, this is a word that falls into the category of deceptive simplicity.

Before moving on to these seven key terms, however, a few observations on Thérèse's language and style are called for, followed by a note on one of her most surprising characteristics, her anti-Jansenism.

LANGUAGE AND STYLE

After some forty centuries of verbal civilization, language has become an exhausted currency. Its strength has been sapped by the lies, bombast, and cunning of horde after horde of invaders. It has been weakened by Greek subtlety and Roman rhetoric, corrupted by medieval chancelleries and by the circumvention of the moderns. Finally, the language of our democracies and dictatorships has saturated the market until the words we use are as inconsistent as stocks and shares. Language has even devalued devotion. Think of all the glib words that believers so easily use when talking about either the greatest love possible or the greatest sin. Our poor battered human language can no longer do its real work: to utter the simple truth.

Thérèse gives a new value to the coinage of words. What she says is what she does. Her words are incontrovertibly authentic.

I use the term "words" to distinguish them from any larger, planned linguistic structure. The overall framework and style of Thérèse's writing is imperfect. This was because of the weakness of those from whom she inherited a mediocre prose style. The French writers of the seventeenth and eighteenth centuries especially wrote with extraordinary precision and accuracy. Men and women alike spoke with an exactitude that rejected pomposity, vagueness, and sheer verbosity. Their heir, the scholar and historian Ernest Renan (1823-92), author of *The Life of Jesus*, tells us that his sister Henrietta saved him from rhetoric and taught him to express himself directly. But, in general, nineteenth-century religious circles had been contaminated by Romanticism. They believed that the proper expression of religious sentiments demanded a style replete with all the impressive devices and sublimity needed to imitate the fine feelings proper to ethereally beautiful souls.

Of course, there is another apparent inadequacy in Thérèse's writing: her fondness for the diminutive. To say "lambkin" for lamb, and "flowerlet" instead of flower (which is really what happens in French, though the usual English "little lamb" and "little flower" do not sound quite so bad) could prove far too tempting and easy a way of invoking the atmosphere of the nursery chatter and dainty verses of infancy. If all that was necessary to create a poetic atmosphere were to use these artless diminutives, as not a few people believed in the sixteenth century, it would be easy to be a poet. If all you had to do to recreate a child's mind and approach was (like Gulliver) to reduce the proportions of objects, to speak of the "poor wee things" and not of the poor, to stick the adjective "little" in front of everything, so that even Daddy becomes "dear little Daddy" and brother "dear little brother," this far too easy device would reduce everything to banality. Her insistence on using diminutives is a feature of Thérèse's vocabulary that remained unchanged from the family circle where she was always the little sister.

Yet here again Thérèse is unique. Whereas in other cases the use of the diminutive is either ridiculous or has no value whatsoever, by some miracle in the work of St Thérèse it suits her message admirably, as long as one comes to understand the growth of its underlying significance throughout her life. If detached from context and the totality of her work, of course, some of her phraseology can sound just as awful as elsewhere.

Thérèse's use of language also shows us what she would have been like if she had never written but had only spoken what she had to say. One might even say that when we hear her talking aloud in her writings, and in her really direct lyrical moments, she becomes the superb stylist that she never really was in any consistent sense. She sometimes quite surprises us by inventing words. For example, she is especially good at coining words ending in "ize" that exactly hit off what she is talking about, as when she describes some "melancholizing" military music, or remarks that St Cecilia's self-abandonment has the capacity to "virginize" souls. When writing verse, Thérèse had a similar sense of sound values. It even, at times, reached the same degree of perfection that Paul Valéry, that twentieth-century master of sonority matched to meaning in poetry, so admired in the dramatic verse of Racine. If she had been more literary, or Racine had been recommended reading in the convent, he would have been a useful model and could have helped her to avoid the occasional insipidity and wrong quantity.

An important feature of the language of much profound discourse, especially when offering spiritual advice, is that it should be short and pithy. A lengthy exposition does not help to get the point home, unless you are St John of the Cross. Thérèse could never have written extended commentaries to help put over the meaning of her own spiritual recommendations, as St John of the Cross did. In fact, much of what she had to say in this respect does not bear commentary as it is so straightforward anyway. In one account of her life, the author says of a confessor's words to her: "He did not repeat them, but there was no need. She had got the point. She always took the point when she was offered help or advice, as if it was a short, clear instruction heard in action." The same was true when she herself gave the help and offered the advice.

Thérèse always teaches "her" way with astonishing assurance and authority for one so young and scarcely well-educated. This particular characteristic of speaking with absolute authority in spite of inexperience reminds us of Joan of Arc. Thérèse is a child yet no child in a world past childhood. The authority with which she speaks is in keeping with her lack of knowledge. If she had known as much as so many others, she would have needed a correspondingly long time to forget it all. If she had exceeded the actual level of her knowledge she would have been liable to devalue this or that Doctor of the Church by some inadequate exposition, or would have merely repeated somewhat tediously what she had learned, and would then have been very much less her own true self. In an age when reaching the masses probably demands detachment from culture and learning, Thérèse's simple, straightforward, and natural writing is a precious model.

Thérèse followed *The Imitation of Christ*, that powerful epitome of, and direct course in, the ascetic and mystical tradition up to the fifteenth century, as well as the seed of many future forms of spirituality. (Her favourite chapters, inasmuch as she refers to them in her writings, were Book I: chapters 1, 2, and 15; Book II: chapter 11; and Book III: chapters 5, 13, 24, 26, 43, 44, 49). She had certainly read these lines:

> Those for whom all things are one
> and the same thing,
> Who know how to relate everything
> to this single thing,
> And who see everything in this unique thing,
> They can have a steadfast heart
> And live peacefully in God.
> O Truth, God of Truth,
> Make me one with you
> In perfect love!

To some, of course, the original Latin will always seem stronger, more resonant and concise:

> *Cui omnia unum sunt*
> *et qui omnia ad unum trahit*
> *et omnia in uno videt*
> *potest stabilis corde esse*
> *et in Deo pacificus permanere*
> *O Veritas Dei, fac me unum tecum*
> *in caritate perfecta!*

THÉRÈSE'S ANTI-JANSENISM

One striking feature common to these texts is their anti-Jansenism.

It is very surprising, given the atmosphere of the times, to find not a hint of even latent Jansenism in the Martin family compared with other Catholic families in the same sector of the French middle class of that period.

Apart from the bastion of extreme Jansenism at Port-Royal itself, the atmosphere of the seventeenth century was permeated with a more diffuse form of Jansenism. It was to be found in the great preacher Bossuet himself, and little by little it seeped into the very fabric of French Catholic culture and life.

One might call this second form a kind of quasi-Jansenism, which went hand-in-hand with what, again, can only be called quasi-Christianity.

From a doctrinal point of view, this secondary form of Jansenism did not go so far as to adopt certain untenable views of grace held by Calvin and Saint-Cyran. As if by way of compensation, and even out of a kind of wilful melancholia, the space thus left free was occupied by apprehension, anxiety, and fear. The same phenomenon has recurred throughout the history of Christianity. Once heresies are banished, emotional but formally permissible reflections of some heretical tenets tend to take the place of the forbidden doctrines. You can certainly prohibit a heresy, but you cannot get rid of a certain inclination in human nature so easily. When a certain kind of doctrine is rejected, a corresponding temperament seems to take its revenge. Those who share it tend to select an as yet uncondemned idea rather like whatever has been anathemized.

This happened with Arianism, which was followed by a semi-orthodox Arianism. Doctrinally speaking, semi-orthodox Jansenism consisted of accepting the notion of the chosen few as the most probable and appropriate of the similar ideas that were still around in the Church. But if the chosen few are so very, very few, what chance have I, an ordinary Christian— or this "little soul," to borrow Thérèse's vocabulary—of being among the elect? What else can I do then, other than retreat into a kind of horribly tense (or totally relaxed) version of quietism, imagining that it is still possible to love God even in hell, and that there is nothing to do but push self-abandonment to a point in a dismal wasteland beyond even the confines of the whole dreary set of beliefs or, rather, psychological inclinations.

Obviously, the majority of Christians did not go to these extremes. But nineteenth-century French piety did include an atmosphere, indebted to this quasi-Jansenism of the previous century and more, which somehow encouraged ideas of this kind. In one way or another, they were much more prevalent than outward conformity would lead one to think. God loves us, but there is always a greater chance of displeasing than of pleasing him. The Christian life is an impossibility for a man of the world. Preaching should awaken and play on worries and anxiety. Only very religious people, and above all religious, can live a perfect religious life. Married women are less assured of their salvation than nuns. Although marriage is tolerated, it can harm the inner life of the soul and is always liable to make us prisoners of the flesh. The world where we have to live is a land where we wait in exile; chronological time is a currency with which we can buy eternity but it has no intrinsic value. Suffering is our essential daily bread. Sickness is a more natural state. Lust is a pit to the edge of which we are ineluctably drawn yet, once we are in it, from which there is no escape except by grace. Heaven is a place of glory without any relation to this earth, which remains a place of sin.

Seven Key Terms

1: LOVE OF THE HUMAN CONDITION

"We only have this life in which to live our faith" (CSG 154).

"We only have the fleeting moments of our life in which to love Jesus" (LT 92).

"There is only one thing to do during the night, the unique night of life, which will only occur once, that is to love and above all to love Jesus . . ." (LT 96).

"I don't see what more I could do after death. . . . I will see the good God, it is true, but as for being with him, I am already completely with him on earth" (DE 15.5.7).

"I have wanted not to see the good God and the saints and to stay in the darkness of faith more than others want to see and understand" (DE 11.8.5).

These paradoxical statements imply that the state of this present life is valuable and desirable. Of course we should not ascribe to Thérèse a belief that the search is superior to possession of what is sought after, or that the means is to be preferred to the end, or the shadow to the light which casts it! But she does say, I am sure, that the quest is a potential attainment of the objective; that the means anticipate the end and enable the aspirant to reach it in some minor way; and that the shadow has its own comfort, when it is cast by God. She also says, of course, that faith is a noble undertaking because it enables love to emerge in the course of believing, which is always a venture.

It is precisely this act of courage which allows her to apprehend and value the benefits of living now, which spiritual people sometimes tend to undervalue.

As a child, she saw a flash of lightning and wrote: ". . . soon, the storm started to growl, the flashes of lightning crisscrossed the sombre clouds, and I heard a clap of thunder in the distance. Far from being frightened I was delighted, as it seemed that the good God was so close to me! . . . " (A 14v).

On another occasion, when she had watched Mother Geneviève die, she wrote this amazing sentence: "It was the first time that I had witnessed a death, it was truly a beatific sight . . ." (A 78v).

To reassure her sister, who was frightened of dying, she wrote in the same vein: "The good God will drink you up like a little drop of dew . . ." (DE 7.4).

In another surprising passage, she speaks of her temptations to reject any notion of the soul surviving after death, and explains how she managed to make these dark thoughts a reason for elation: "I think of myself as an unfledged chick, and certainly not as an eagle. But somehow, even though I am so feeble, my heart's eyes have taken in the eagle's stratagem of staring at the sun, the sun of divine love. Of course the poor fledgling can't hope to copy those eagles, the great souls who fly straight to the throne of the Blessed Trinity. All it can do is flap its wings in a vain attempt to fly. You would suppose then that all it could do is to die of disappointment on finding itself so useless. But I don't worry about all that. I remain where I am and keep my eyes on the sun. . . . I know that it is still there behind the clouds, as bright as ever. Sometimes, it is true, the heart of this little bird is battered by a storm, and I find it difficult to believe that anything at all exists except for the clouds surrounding me. This is the moment of PERFECT JOY. . . . If dark clouds have hidden the star of Love, the little bird does not move, it knows that its sun is still shining behind the clouds. . . ." (B 5r).

2: A SENSE OF REALITY

"Truth is my only nourishment" (DE 5.8.4).

"Enlighten me. You know that I am searching for truth" (B 4v.)

We constantly notice evidence of this spirit of truth in

Thérèse. She is always anxious for its inspiration, and finds nourishment only where there is no exaggeration, legend or pomposity. She did not have the kind of critical education that would have enabled her to tell by the exercise of her own judgment what was authentic and what was false. But she obviously possessed a natural critical faculty which, if she had been well-educated, would have made sure that someone of her intelligence looked for truth where it was to be found and shunned fictions. The same is true of Joan of Arc, who was neither theologian nor casuist, and who was illiterate in the conventional sense. Yet the answers she gave at her trial enable us to guess at what might be called her "theologal" intelligence, at her astonishing ability to analyze and resolve the conundrums she was faced with; this faculty, if it had been developed, would have been equal to the greatest.

For example, when Thérèse spoke about the Virgin Mary during her last illness, she said: "For a sermon on the Holy Virgin to please me and do me good, I have to see her REAL life rather than her supposed life."

The texts that she discovered, selected, and copied out from the Bible are very remarkable. Probably only someone with a very well-informed and acute intellect could have made such pertinent choices: Psalm 22 (*Dominus regit me et nihil mihi deerit*: "The Lord is my shepherd; I shall not want . . ."); chapter 53 of Isaiah on the suffering Servant ("He is despised and rejected of men; a man of sorrows, and acquainted with grief; and we hid as it were our faces from him; he was despised, and we esteemed him not . . ."); The Sermon on the Mount; chapter 17 of John's Gospel ("I have glorified thee on earth; I have finished the work which thou gavest me to do . . ."); chapters 12 and 13 of First Corinthians ("Now concerning spiritual gifts, brethren, I would not have you ignorant . . ."; "Though I speak with the tongues of men and of angels, and have not charity, I am become as sounding brass, or a tinkling cymbal . . .").

Accordingly, she strove for a form of holiness without "any illusions" (A 78r).

Thérèse's desire for truth was a perennial theme in her works and conversation, and was evident from a very young age. It is possible to reconstruct her entire spirituality on the basis of the idea of truth and of self-knowledge, which has been an essential philosophic theme since Socrates. Because she knows herself so well, even in the innermost depths of her being, she tolerates no overstatement of any kind, even for pious ears. This notion of truth enables her, though just a child, to rise above the theology, mysticism, and exegesis of her time. This understanding of truth gives her style such force, even though she was neither a naturally-gifted nor an accomplished writer or poet. This concept of truth makes her sympathetic to the best in all sorts and conditions of people. It sets her apart from so many other saints who, however holy in their particular form of sanctity, stand for received religious opinions. Yet nothing is so simple, direct, sublime, and true as Thérèse's last known statement: "Yes, it seems to me that I have never looked for anything but the truth!" (DE 30.9).

She was never attracted by improbable stories. With regard to Jesus' infancy, she said: "What makes me feel good when I think of the Holy Family is when I think of their living ordinary lives. Neither all that we are told nor what people suppose actually happened. For example, the story that the Child Jesus made some clay birds, blew over them and gave them life . . . No, no, little Jesus never performed useless miracles." (DE 20.8.14).

A nun told her that when she died the angels would come to accompany her to heaven: "All these images," replied the Saint, "do nothing for me. Truth is my only nourishment. That's why I never wanted to have visions. . . . I would prefer to wait until after my death" (DE 5.8.4).

3. GOD'S DISLIKE OF HUMAN SUFFERING

"God who loves us so much is sufficiently troubled about leaving us on this earth to suffer our time of trial, without our constantly hurrying to tell him that we're unhappy here. We should behave as if we didn't notice it!" (CSG 58).

This pronouncement of Thérèse's seems very odd indeed, if we compare what she says with conventional opinions on the subject. The vocabulary of suffering has become so familiar in Western theology that it might seem that God, without really enjoying man's suffering, wants it for its own sake. Pascal, after all, offered the quite ghastly proposition that sickness was the natural state of a Christian, who ought to be shocked at finding himself or herself in good health.

Thérèse's remark does indeed imply a new attitude to suffering among Christians. It is not that St Thérèse was asking for a life full of easy options. As we know, she always accepted her full share of austerity and painful striving in religion. She had so strong a special devotion to the crucified face of our Lord that she even included it in her name in religion—as Thérèse of the Child Jesus and of the Holy Face. One might say that her short life was a series of trials, the most painful of which was her father's paralysis, before she was finally diagnosed as a consumptive. But she did not associate a salvific value with this suffering, as suffering, as Christians are often inclined to do, and as the enemies of Christianity are particularly fond of criticizing them for doing. For Thérèse, suffering was a means to an end. Her attitude was in line with St Paul's profound idea in Philippians and Hebrews: that Christ's suffering is a consequence of his obedience to his Father: "Christ Jesus . . . though he was in the form of God, did not count equality with God a thing to be grasped, but emptied himself, taking the form of a servant, being born in the likeness of men. And being found in human form he humbled himself and became obedient unto death, even death on a cross . . . whatever gain I had, I counted as loss for the sake of Christ.

31

Indeed I count everything as loss because of the surpassing worth of knowing Christ Jesus my Lord. For his sake I have suffered the loss of all things, and count them as refuse, in order that I may gain Christ and be found in him, not having a righteousness of my own, based on law, but that which is through faith in Christ, the righteousness from God that depends on faith; that I may know him and the power of his resurrection, and may share his sufferings, becoming like him in his death, that if possible I may obtain the resurrection from the dead" (Phil. 2:5-8; 3:7-11). Christ's sufferings are not imposed on us because there is an intrinsic merit in suffering for its own sake. But, after the Fall, suffering (which enables us to offer God our disinterested loyalty and redeem our wrong use of freedom) represents a kind of short-cut to the right attitude to, and an eventual confrontation with, our death and destiny. God who sees and accepts this suffering, views and wants it much as one would see and accept medicine or surgery. And this violent expedient is so temporary, and above all so minor, compared to what it ensures, which belongs to another order altogether: which is eternal, happy, and unchanging. We must also take into account the fact that her sister condensed Thérèse's thinking on evil into this strikingly rigorous and Virgilian image: God suffers from as well as suffers our suffering; he suffers it to affect us while looking away from our suffering.

From this point of view, the Christian God is a God not of vengeance but of eternal Love. He is our wise mentor who, far from increasing our hardship, tries to cut it short, suspend it, and reduce it as much as is divinely possible. He does so in order to satisfy his justice, which is paradoxically identical with the glory he wants us to enjoy.

We are a long way here from the idea of the "valley of tears," but also from the "shower of roses," which a superficial reader of St Thérèse might suppose she wanted her friends to experience always. We have passed beyond the stage of these two metaphors familiar to all readers of the saint's basic works and story. Now, with Thérèse, we are in a position to understand the deep meaning of suffering and to measure it by the yardstick of divine judgment.

In this remark of Thérèse's we find the teaching of Peter and Paul in a very simple, straightforward form. I am thinking of the occasions when, though not jointly, and from very different basic standpoints, they maintain that the sufferings of this time cannot be set against the everlasting weight of glory, or that we must suffer present trials and sorrows for a short space, because the outcome is so immeasurably momentous and beneficial.

We can find the same notion in St Luke's account of the risen Jesus, when the Lord talks to his disciples on the way to Emmaus. Jesus makes no reference to the cross as a transient, fleeting event, of course, but the three companions are quite aware of the rapidity of the whole sequence, for the Thursday before there was no question of it at all. Jesus reminds them of the way and law of all flesh and all spirit: "Was it not necessary that the Messiah should suffer these things and then enter into his glory?" (Luke 24:26).

When we recall the objections of rationalism, humanism, and Communism to Christian doctrine as inimical to human happiness, the relevance of Thérèse's mysticism should become immediately apparent.

Suffering is not the work of God, of the good God, of the Father from whom all good things flow; it is the product of sin, the fruit of original sin. God's mercy and loving-kindness transform this bitter fruit into an "ennobling" remedy. God is already rejoicing at our anticipation of the everlasting health we are intended to enjoy. "This idea makes me much happier," writes Thérèse. "Now I understand why he lets us suffer!"

"The suffering of this world cannot compare with the future glory which will be shown to us," says St Paul. "O Cross, my life's sweet resting-place!" exclaims Teresa of Avila.

Nevertheless, at the end of her life Thérèse was able to pass beyond this penchant she had for trials. After all, to choose the cross still means wanting something, and replacing God's with our own desire. A generous and courageous soldier can ask for a dangerous mission, but a hazardous sortie might prejudice the general welfare and the successful outcome of a vast campaign, and those who enjoy dangerous glory should resign themselves to the monotonous existence of obscure combatants, as so often happens in wars, in which tedium is a greater threat to the spirit than physical danger. Thérèse managed to rise above the condition of making any such choice. Toward the end, she expressed how she felt thus: "Now I no longer have any desire other than LOVING Jesus to the point of madness. It is only LOVE that attracts me. . . . I no longer desire either suffering or death, yet I like them both! I have wanted them for a long time. . . . But now, it is only the act of total surrender which guides me, I have no other compass! I am no longer able to ask for anything passionately except the perfect fulfillment for my soul of what God wants . . ." (A 83r).

4: THE WORK OF THIS WORLD CONTINUED IN HEAVEN

"I want to spend my time in heaven doing good on earth. . . . This is not impossible, because the angels watch over us in the very heart of the beatific vision" (DE 17.7).

"I count on not staying inactive in heaven. I want to go on working for the Church and for souls. . . . Surely the Angels are continually looking after us, while never taking their eyes from the face of God. . . . Dear Brother, you will see that if I have already left the battlefield, it is not because I have any selfish desire to rest, for the thought of eternal blessedness hardly brings a flutter to my heart. For a long while suffering has become my Heaven here below and I really find it difficult to understand how I could get used to a Country where joy reigns without any

admixture of sadness. Jesus will have to transform my soul and make it able to enjoy things . . ." (LT 254).

"The thought of celestial happiness not only gives me no joy, but I still wonder sometimes how it will be possible for me to be happy without suffering. No doubt Jesus will change my nature, otherwise I would regret the suffering and the valley of tears" (LT 258).

These astonishing passages about human love are almost disturbing and extraordinarily modern.

In order to comment on them appropriately, I can only choose Dmitri Merezhkovsky as my guide. As a young man he knew Dostoievsky and revived his tradition. Merezhkovsky believed that Joan of Arc and Thérèse of the Child-Jesus were both original thinkers who wanted heaven on earth, yet were not trying to pretend that the world could be heaven but, on the contrary, to bring down heaven on earth.

The far-sighted and subtly associative Merezhkovsky brought the centuries together and even reversed them, almost to the point of identifying the two virgin saints as one and the same person. When he wrote about them, of course, neither of them was a patron of France (I have condensed the original text to a certain extent, and toned down its typically Russian apocalyptical tone, to emphasize the points that concern us here):

> If France was really saved by Joan, so was the whole of Europe. The salvation or the ruin of France, the most vital part of the European body, meant the life or death of the whole body. This truth seems very obvious to us in the twentieth century and Joan tried to bring it home to the fifteenth century. Of these two great saints—one who emerged in the Christian France of the past, and the other who lived in the dechristianized France of our own times—St Joan of Arc and St Thérèse of Lisieux, the latter resembles the former as little as the twentieth century the fifteenth. But surely, like Thérèse, Joan could have said:

"I want to spend my time in heaven doing good on earth." Thérèse expressed her religious experience with great precision; Joan lived it out in silence (but more profoundly perhaps than any other great saint). They are like one another not only because of a determination to live and act their faith as human beings on this earth, which was the very source of their sanctity, but because they comprise one and the same soul in two bodies: they are France that is past and France that is to come. From this world toward the other world; from earth to heaven: the way of all the saints is an upward path. But Joan and Thérèse move in the other direction, descending from heaven toward earth, from the other world to this one. This sanctity in reverse originates in the odd fact that it was not the world-renouncing Church but the Church-abandoning world that first acknowledged and fell in love with these two saints. Both loved the world dominated by evil, and were loved by the world. A few days before her death, Thérèse had a prophetic dream. Because they were running out of soldiers for a great war, somebody said: "We'll have to send Sister Thérèse!"—"I replied that I would really have preferred being recruited for a holy war," but she was sent off all the same. After describing this dream, she exclaimed: "How very happy I would have been to go to war, during the crusades for example! Just think of it! I wouldn't have been scared of stopping a bullet! [*sic*] Do you think I shall really die in bed?" (DE 4.8.6 and 7.) (*From Jesus to Us*, pp. 378-81).

Merezhkovsky was convinced that Joan and Thérèse were the two most modern and revolutionary saints of a revolution that has hardly begun and will take us into a new age.

When Thérèse tried to think of heaven, she could conceive of it only as a place that would allow her to be loving to people.

Thérèse Martin counted on still being active and working effectively in the after-life. She had no desire to start "being at rest" or "at peace," which is the sort of existence that we wish on people who are dead when we talk about them. What she wanted was not *Requiem aeternam dona nobis Domine* ("Give us eternal rest, O Lord") but, on the contrary, *Actionem aeternam dona nobis Domine* ("Give us eternal action, O Lord!") or, more exactly in her case: "My God, give me the power to act eternally with you!"

For St Thérèse, heaven was a place of continuous action of an angelic kind. She thought that from the moment of death she would be a kind of knight in shining armour, and begin to carry out her duties as an Angel of God like that. The solemn moment would not be the time when she would "enter on" her eternal rest, but the start of an eternity of unlimited activity. Life in the body, after all, imposed bounds on her actions and prevented her from fulfilling her vocation of universal charity in any other way than by offering up her lonely heart in the closed world of the Carmel of Lisieux.

Now this boundless love, this vocation to enjoy and practise all vocations, would be fulfilled. Thérèse's love, once released from all trammels and restraints, could reach out to all points in space, adapt to all the circumstances of the problem, and answer all the needs of the Church's missions.

*   *   *

In order to understand this very personal aspect of Thérèse proficiently, it may be helpful to compare her with Bd Elizabeth of the Trinity.

Elizabeth imitated the spirit of the beloved disciple. She may be said to have based her prayers on Jesus' discourse after the Last Supper in John's Gospel. Her active and passive spirituality was concerned with the indwelling in our souls of God the Father and Son.

Thérèse, on the other hand, was closer to the spirit of St Paul, with his burning desire to extend the vitality and unity of the body of Christ among human beings, to satisfy all vocations, to move and spread throughout all possible space, and to accomplish all missions.

Elizabeth was more inclined to follow the solitary way of St John of the Cross, who was particularly concerned to purify his soul, and to let it be transformed by God.

Our Thérèse was in many ways a worthy spiritual successor of her earlier namesake of Avila, though without the added quality of the Spanish saint's ecstatic mysticism.

As in all comparisons between two souls remarkable for their universality, the differences are only those of degree. Elizabeth declared that she too would have a mission in heaven: to help people to emerge from the confines of their own former selves, and to care for them in the silent stretches of infinity. Thérèse, however, thought of heavenly existence as a celebration of God. Each could easily adopt the other's other secondary or complementary traits. Their essential similarity is not cancelled because Elizabeth felt that she was summoned to enter a very celestial heaven, which would have absorbed all thought of this world:

> I plunge into Infinity,
> Dive into my patrimony.
> In this profound immensity,
> As in eternity,
> My soul is blessed.
> With the Trinity I rest.

From this point of view she is in the great, "conventional" tradition of mysticism. Thérèse is somewhat more revolutionary.

When Elizabeth was asked how she was going to "spend her eternity" and if, like Thérèse, she would "come back" to earth, she replied: "Certainly not! The moment I reach the threshold of eternity I shall be off like a shot into the heart of the Trinity, where I shall be irremovable."

5: PURGATORY, A REALM OF LOVE

"If I go to Purgatory, I shall be very happy. I shall do what the three Hebrews did in the fiery furnace: I shall walk through the flames singing the canticle of Love" (DE 7.8.15).

"If you only knew how gentle God will be with me!" (DE 7.8.15).

"As for children, they will be judged very, very kindly" (DE 25.9.1).

The notion of "the chosen few," the "predestination" of Jansenism, and some versions of what is known as "quietism" are branches from the same trunk. If the likelihood of my salvation is very minimal, I should like to be reassured at any price. The doctrine of predestination may be helpful in this respect, for it says that each member of the elect is already chosen from all eternity by divine decree, without any reference to an individual's actual merits. Surely, then, I have every reason to hope that I am numbered among the company of God's elect? And if I am numbered among the legions of the condemned, well, so what, quietism says that I shall enjoy a kind of final rest anyway. Even at the centre of hell, so it seems, I shall be able to give God some signs of "pure love."

Thérèse pared all these more or less morbid images down to their roots.

She thought that people of good will would be judged favourably on Judgment Day. Her words in this respect reproduce the angelic salutation: "Peace on earth to men of good will!"

She did not try to reclaim, and did not usually show a special interest in, obdurate criminals, but Pranzini was an exception. He was condemned to death for the murder of two women and a child; he had killed them in the course of theft. Thérèse prayed for him. Just before he was executed, having previously refused any religious advice or consolation, he suddenly cried out: "Quick, the crucifix!" and kissed it. Her experience of the apparent effects of prayer in this case seemed to show that an obstinate sinner, whose appalling crimes certainly seemed to have destined him for eternal damnation, could still be saved even at the last moment.

Now that her childlike soul had successfully interceded for an obvious candidate for damnation, and had enabled him to pass in an instant from "death to life" by virtue of an act of love, Thérèse thought that all souls could do the same thing. After all, a miracle is only a special insight that the human mind and soul are granted into the overall creative work of God (which never stops, even though we are not so directly, blindingly aware of its continuity, and of every particular, always miraculous, example of its effects). Thérèse experienced the miracle that she was convinced resulted from her prayer and mortification on behalf of this condemned man as a revelatory flash of illumination, an immediate insight into the whole work of universal redemption.

The day after Pranzini's execution she read the account of his sudden change of heart in the newspaper *La Croix*. Yes, there was an obvious causal relationship between her own humble act of sacrifice and the criminal's unexpected final repentance. This event had a radical effect on her thinking. We are rarely given direct evidence—or rather evidence that we are willing and able to understand—of the fulfilment of the solemn promise repeated seven times during Jesus' discourse after the Last Supper: "Very truly, I tell you, if you ask anything of the Father in my name, he will give it to you" (John 16:23). Yet it is a fundamental principle of that mysterious realm which lies beyond our immediate earthbound perception.

Thérèse never went so far as to say that no one could ever possibly go to hell. She did not deny that damnation was a terrifying possibility for human beings. Yet, in one particular instance, and on one particular occasion in her own life and experience, she had sensed and felt the effects of the complex and mysterious power exercised by what she and we know as the Communion of Saints.

Because she was convinced that even the greatest sinner could be saved, there was now all the more reason for believing in the salvation of people of good will, whom she endearingly termed "little souls." Traditional thinking held that no one knew if he or she was worthy of love or hate; without actually rejecting it, Thérèse replaced this view with one that was more reassuring and truthful: "No one knows whether he or she is a just person or a sinner, but Jesus gives us the grace to feel in the depths of our hearts that we would rather die than offend him." One day, at her school (run by Benedictines), she was heard to say (speaking especially of infants who had died unbaptized, and who many theologians and general Catholic belief claimed could never enjoy the beatific vision, and "had to be" excluded from God's presence in a strictly mundane place of dubious bliss known as Limbo): "If I were God, I believe that I would save everyone."

It would be interesting to know all Thérèse's thoughts about the overall related, and problematical, subject of unequal gifts of grace. Consideration of the lives of various individuals, the life of the Church, and her own family circle, must have shown her (what the gospel says anyway) that God is master of his gifts and that he gives more to one than to another. After all, to put something infinitely mysterious into the rather banal language proper to human affairs, which will make God seem both as arbitrary and as subject to legal constraints as are human beings, we may say that what God bestows is entirely within his own gift. He gives more to one than to another. This sounds paradoxical, but the whole subject of the unequal distribution of the gifts of God's infinite bounty is paradoxical, for paradox is our wholly inadequate term for the unknowable mind of God. What at first seems the perfectly reasonable objection of the labourers in the vineyard, who have suffered the heat of the day yet receive the same wages as those hired just before sundown, is quite unreasonable if we try to translate God's action into terms proper to

41

human legality, and make a distinction between the divine justice which God "has to" exercise and the loving-kindness with which he gives whomsoever he wishes whatsoever he, God, thinks and therefore knows is appropriate.

Yet any act of preference for one person rather than another seems to wound one person or another, and to affect the purity of love. Of course it is possible not to envy a brother who is the sole heir to a fortune. Nevertheless, if two brothers receive unequal shares of their father's property, it is difficult to think that their relationship will ever be the same again.

One rather unusual nineteenth-century Christian thinker, Jules Lequier, centred his work on an exhaustive examination of this problem. In one of his most profound pieces, *Abel and Abel*, he showed that those who seem to have received less in life have really received more, because "God gives those whom he deprives of gifts something far richer than those whom he gives more to." Lequier bases his argument on the supposition that there are twin brothers, Abel and Abel, whom God loves equally. But God has given one of them a unique gift. Three hypotheses follow. Two are jealousy and the privileged Abel's surrender of his legacy to his less fortunate brother. Lequier felt that these two solutions were imperfect. The true solution is that the deprived Abel begs his brother to accept the situation of having more, and consoles him for having been favoured in this way. Lequier tries to show that a kind of striving to the point of a total equilibrium of love comes about between the Abel who receives the inheritance and the Abel who does not, so that each consoles the other for his misfortune.

This somewhat unfathomable view appears several times in Thérèse's writings, especially in the (deceptively subtle) logic that enabled her to tell the Virgin Mary: "You have everything, yet you are infinitely deprived because you do not have a heavenly Mother to love, since you are that Mother yourself."

"O, Mary, if I were the Queen of Heaven and you were Thérèse, I would want to be Thérèse so that you would be Queen of Heaven!" (Pr. 21, 8.9.1897).

We know that she wrote these statements (which I shall comment on shortly) three weeks before her death.

Whoever deciphers their meaning correctly must accept and even love his or her earthly state. Here, yet again, we encounter Thérèse's idea (which is so novel in the history of Western religious feeling and spirituality) that, in spite of all its precariousness and fragility, the human condition, the life of faith, is actually enviable.

Further reflection on this point will show that something like the same idea is present in the Creation and above all in the Incarnation. But it would be necessary to write at great length to demonstrate these implications which are so clearly enunciated in Thérèse's few words.

Thérèse has the remarkable ability to show us that purgatory is not a place of anguished pain. Rather like St Catherine of Genoa, she re-thinks the whole meaning of purgatory in the light of love. Essentially, anyone in purgatory is following a path that is the way of the highest form of mystical life, in the midst of all the trials of this state of purification. The fire of purgatory is a fire of joy; whereas hell-fire is a fire of torment.

We are always wrapped in the love of God. Our own attitude to that love can change it into fire or light. Once in purgatory, people are necessarily contemplatives. They have to undergo an experience of total darkness, similar to the dark night of the soul experienced by the great mystics and even by Our Lady, although she was without sin. But the difference between the great mystics, still on earth and struggling with a kind of uncertainty about their final end, and the souls in purgatory is that the latter do not have the same worry. They are already "in the hands of God"; they already walk through the "flames" like the loving children in the fiery furnace. Even though waiting to be freed is painful for them, and more acutely so as their time of release approaches (I can vouch for this on the basis of my experience as a former prisoner-of-war), at least they are granted absolute certainty: they are in eternity, and are on the right course. They are no longer aware of what Newman in *Gerontius*, his poem about purgatory, called "the busy beat of time." Freed from their biological bodies and their social obligations, and even from all their worries and responsibilities, they belong entirely to God, are all in God, and are all for God. It is even conceivable that they would not want their period in purgatory to be shortened, because they are wholly taken up by the love of the will of God. St Catherine of Genoa (author of a treatise on purgatory, but probably unknown to Thérèse, in spite of similarities between them) said that the souls in purgatory were happy in their suffering, if they were able to ignore themselves; and that they were not even able to torture themselves with the fruitless regret that they had not lived holier lives. As Thérèse thought, in the midst of all the purification they are undergoing (whatever form that may take) there must be a deep layer of peace and serenity in the intermediary state of purgatory. For us "poor sinners," who hardly dare hope to be admitted directly to the Beatific Vision, it is a joy to know that in this place of pure development, we shall be secure in a state of pure love, and freed from the only anguish that is really terrifying: that of being able to do wrong and any longer being people who would do wrong.

6: EFFORTLESS EFFORT

"I shall be near you, holding your hand, so that it can effortlessly pick the palm of martyrdom" (LT 254).

"The rattle of the machine-gun and cannon's roar mean nothing when one is supported by the General" (LT 200).

"To shut my eyes, is that too much to ask? Not to have combat the horrors of the night?" (LT 205).

There are many passages of this kind in Thérèse's letters and pronouncements, but their really up-to-date and vitally incisive nature has perhaps been misunderstood.

Sometimes the most luminous and pithy sayings need no commentary to tease out their implications. Others, like these, do. Sometimes "geniuses" offer advice in a curiously unknowing way. The problem is that you can't really imitate a genius. If Raphael had said (as he did, in effect): "Do as I do, do what you have to do effortlessly. It comes out best when you're just not thinking about what you're doing," his advice would be rather useless to most young would-be artists.

In Thérèse's somewhat different case, the paradoxical operation of "genius," "childhood," or "grace" similarly makes otherwise difficult actions appear simple and natural. Such privileged people often tell us to imitate them without taking into account that we would have to work to and beyond the limits of all capabilities to achieve an effect equivalent to that produced by a God-given facility. When Thérèse said: "Do as I do. Imitate the Child," it is tantamount to saying: "Do as I do: be a genius." She obviously found it very difficult to see how hard it is to follow an easy road.

Nevertheless, these recommendations to follow the way of non-effort contain a deep truth which modern psychology, and psychoanalysis in particular, has highlighted.

To summarize these suggestions (I am thinking especially of the excellent work of Abramowsky and Charles Baudoin on suggestion and auto-suggestion, but above all of Alain's constant advice in his short essays for a wider public about discarding prejudices and rethinking everything for yourself), we might say that in reality there are two kinds of effort. For a long time they were confused with one another. There is the sort of effort that contracts one's forces, and draws one into oneself. This merely serves to increase the obduracy of the difficulty, as one sometimes sees in sales-people, but also in shy, withdrawn persons.

This type of striving (Alain rightly says that someone who

makes an effort in this sense is working against himself or herself) is a kind of poison generated by the act of volition. If this impulse exceeds its limitations, and we are not on our guard against it, it produces a high degree of nervous tension. It reduces our attention-span, and diminishes our efficiency and effectiveness. Any determination just to ignore a tendency to build up resentment, spleen, and the tight sort of depressive resistance I have in mind not only has the opposite effect of evoking it, but makes it all the stronger and more malevolent. Accordingly, the best way of resisting temptation is distraction or diversion.

This is well-known to all spiritual writers and spiritual directors. But it is important to remember that even any mention of the temptation is dangerous. Valour in this respect is a matter of conscious flight from its very image, for you are lost as soon as you try to fight it in that tense, contracted way that invites it to take hold of you, and gives the image that you actually want to suppress a terrifyingly hallucinatory power over you.

Thérèse often shows her awareness of the advice of St Francis de Sales when she advocates flight, which is the best way of escaping the awful struggle between the will and the image of constraint that it sets up against its own intentions. Her recommendations might well have come from the work of the French psychologist and psychotherapist Emile Coué (1857-1926; who invented a method of healing by auto-suggestion). Thérèse virtually summarizes the beneficial approach of this gifted man, less well-known than Freud, but who could easily have founded a school of psychotherapy at Nancy: "When there is a struggle between the will and a contrary image, the strength of the image grows in proportion to the will-power exerted, and is never less than its square."

For example, if I am frightened and I fight against my fear, I do not reduce but increase it, in ever-growing proportions. Consequently, military leaders do not try to combat their troops' fear but make sure that they keep them occupied. That is why generals often dislike a purely defensive action more than anything.

Of course this does not mean that we should not make an effort. It means that alongside the kind of effort that contracts the will there is a positive, favourable, and admirable kind of effort: one that duly relaxes the will, and which fits the due and proper intention of the effort planned and made. The mystics call this impulse "abandonment," or "self-abandonment." In fact it is an effortless form of effort—effort without effort—which is more difficult to accomplish than effort pure and simple. This ordinary kind of effort requires a "habituation" or customary, even semi-automatic exercise of the will.

"This is something," the philosopher Bergson wrote,

> which has never been subjected to analysis until now, and which is still rather enigmatic. Surely those who have achieved excellence without making any effort, have in fact made an effort, but of a kind quite different from all normal effort. They have made an effort which is not classifiable as instantaneous. We come closest to it if we say that it is like the straightforward process of resolving something, which occurs when we concentrate on that thing, when beforehand, until that process of concentration (when it began to take on a definable shape), we were aware of that thing only in, so to speak, a diffuse form, even though it had a certain kind of duration and extent which made it more than totally vague and inchoate.
>
> Religion, to be sure, would not elevate someone to a position of pre-eminence merely because of that kind of effortless achievement. I certainly do not think that anyone is born perfect. At a given moment there must be some more or less deserved, or "merited," intervention— some form of assistance—from on high.
>
> There are those who achieve this very elevated state by a more or less rapid process of effort on their own part, yet who, when someone else observes them in the course

of their achievement, seem to the observer to have done it just like that, directly, with no effort whatsoever. This is so, even though something corresponding or appropriate to effort as such actually has to go on inside such achievers.

I use the analogy of my own experience as a horseman to illustrate this. As a young man, I loved to go riding. One day I decided to make no effort to do something I had previously put all my effort into. The result was much, much better when I stopped being tense and started to relax and be really confident. But this state is very difficult to analyze; it has to be studied empirically. Anyway I realized that what was involved wasn't courage, because the risk was negligible. Perhaps it was the confidence to entrust myself—but to whom or what? I don't know. Let us say: to the genius of horsemanship, because I do not presume to say: to God. It was a matter of absolute confidence, the almost instantaneous equivalent of a whole series of "efforts," or instances of effort, and gave me suppleness, facility and something else too. To be a good horseman you should start riding early on in life; then you can get there fairly quickly and easily. But those who have made an effort always retain something of the effort they had to make to become successful riders. Some people are natural riders who very quickly acquire perfect, absolute ease on horseback; but only a few are privileged in this way. I had to make an enormous effort; but I felt that I should have been able to achieve the same result without such an effort, and yet there would always have been something that took the place of that effort, and would have subsumed it under some simply deceptive appearance. What is in question here is an indefinable state, an intermediate state between a physical and a mental (or even moral) disposition. If I knew how to analyze it exactly, I would have discovered a way of putting it into effect.

At one level or another, you find evidence of a certain mysterious disposition which operates perfectly in a state of grace. It is met with elsewhere in what, compared with that state, is metaphorical form—but then the metaphor in question conceals something real that can be detected and elucidated by experiment.

Human nature is such that most people have greater confidence in someone who reaches this state smoothly, straightaway, just like that, and who is also naturally honest and sincere, than in someone who makes a hard and painful effort to get there. This is a perceptive judgment, I am sure, because the former must conceal a finer equivalent of the meritorious effort made by the latter. (Cited by Jacques Chevalier in *Entretiens avec Bergson*, 1959).

This is a very interesting and meticulous description of a mysterious state. The second type of effort, which I call "abandonment," possesses what may be called a striking equivalence to effort, just as a piece of gold possesses an equivalence to currency—its monetary value.

St Thérèse wanted her friends to reach this level of effortless effort, which in this regard is analogous to genius. Because of the relationship between the operations of genius and ordinary play, Thérèse was able to develop the habit of representing ascetic practices in (or, rather, translating them into) the language of play, a much more profound activity. This was a commendable psychological or, rather, spiritual device. The word "play" and actual play naturally make us think of something done with ease; and, by representing and acting out effort in the language of play and in the behaviour proper to play, as she did, it is possible to divert, if not to avoid, the tension of burgeoning anxiety, fear, anguish, and so on. I think that St Francis of Assisi's joy, Grignion de Montfort's abandonment, and Joseph Cottolengo's and the Salesians' humour are instances of something very like this particular practice, and not only help practitioners to resolve a very difficult problem in the spiritual life, but help us to understand what they are doing. Above all, thinking along these lines will help us to understand the paradoxes of Thérèse's apparently contradictory or at least gnomic utterances and seemingly odd behaviour. When very much more is generally known about him, St Philip Neri (1515-1595; the founder of the Oratorians) who avoided controversy, lived so simply yet was at the service of all, seemed to have the faculty of influencing and converting individuals by sheer "force of character," and experienced mystical states of rapture when saying Mass, will surely figure as the virtuoso of this type of spiritual effort.

Certainly all these ways of trying to reach the goal "directly" (as Henri Rambaud puts it so neatly: "Excellence takes less effort than mediocrity") can sometimes produce a merely illusory result. Some people think they are geniuses when they are merely on the point of doing the thing (often by the skin of their teeth) just as it ought to be done anyway. Others fondly imagine that mere spontaneity is true genius. Practitioners of the ascetic methods of St Ignatius of Loyola or St Vincent de Paul, based on the *Spiritual Exercises* or the *Practice of a Holy Life*, sometimes convince themselves that their merely repetitive use of these frameworks of devotion entitles them to be classed as geniuses in the spiritual life, when they are grinding along with mere substitutes for the far from rote practice of the real thing.

Thérèse constantly refers to asceticism, of course, and recommends the constant exercise of "infinitesimal" virtues, thus quite unconsciously putting into practice the German philosopher Leibniz's idea of "infinitely small" sacrifices, which has much to do with his analysis of complex truths into simple truths, and of definable terms into indefinable terms, and with his lifelong interest in the resolution of knowledge into fundamental simple ideas. Some interesting related thoughts about Thérèse are also possible on the basis of Leibniz's conception of the after-life: "Supreme felicity, by whatever beatific vision or knowledge of God it may be accompanied, can never be full; for, since God is infinite, he cannot be wholly known. Therefore our happiness will never, and ought not to consist in full joy where there would be nothing to desire, rendering our mind stupid, but in a perpetual progress to new pleasures and to new perfections" (*The Principles of Nature and of Grace*, 18).

7: UNREAL TIME AND THE EVERLASTING MOMENT

"Jesus takes no notice of time, because there isn't any such thing in Heaven" (LT 114).

"Is life a dream then? And to think that we can save souls with a dream like that!" (LT 130).

"Time is nothing but a illusion, a dream. God already sees us in glory, and rejoices that we are blessed for ever" (LT 108).

"Each moment is an eternity, an everlasting joy" (LT 96).

Thérèse's inspiration for her thoughts on the unreality of time was her discovery of the celebrated fifty-third chapter of Isaiah on the suffering Servant. Isaiah's account so long ago of these "hidden beauties of Jesus" made Thérèse rethink her ideas on chronological time. It helped her to see that in God "before" and "after" are contemporary, for she and Isaiah saw Christ in the same way.

"I am thinking about time and wondering what it means exactly," Thérèse wrote to Céline in 1890. She did not know then that St Augustine (354-430) had asked the same question: "Time is nothing but an illusion, a dream . . . God already sees us in glory, and rejoices that we are blessed for ever!" (LT 108).

In itself, this is an extremely daring thought. In a sense, Thérèse the Child is the only one who would dare to state it in this way. She aligns herself directly with the viewpoint of God, in the sense of predestination. Then, with hope undaunted, she includes herself (and her sister, too, it seems) among the elect. It is reminiscent of the question asked of Joan of Arc, which she evaded so adroitly: "If I am not in a state of grace, may God put me in one; if I am, may he keep me there." Joan stayed on a human level with her answer, keeping to our viewpoint of uncertainty, and to our lack of assurance that we actually possess the "gift of perseverance."

But the Child Thérèse boldly assumes the right to unroll the divine plan of eternity and of predestined love. In this plan, she can see herself only as one loved by God, and is aware only of God rejoicing in the blessed state of her soul. Time does not exist and God is love. And she knows that she is in love and is a loving person. Thérèse takes these affirmations to the point of their ultimate implication: God must already be rejoicing in my glory.

Having gone this far, however, she does not fall into the trap of making a further, but false deduction. She does not confuse God's plan, which is on the level of eternity, with human projects, produced by people acting on the level of uncertain chronological time. Anything with a whiff of pre-destination about it could lead to pride and sloth. A person might well say reassuringly: "I am already saved. Therefore I can do what I like, or at least there's no need to make any kind of effort in life."

Thérèse draws quite contradictory conclusions from her excessive trust. If Jesus sees me already in glory, he must want me to deserve what he has given me. Therefore I have to act with my whole being and all my love. May he bring me to "wear the blood-stained robes of a martyr" but "not bargain with me!"

Here we are at the opposite extreme from Pelagius, for whom human effort was the only means of gaining a heavenly reward. For Thérèse, as for St Augustine, grace (apparent as glory), is the primary source of merit.

But the Child Thérèse is all but blithely playing with counters that actually stand for ancient and ultimately unfathomable problems. She has strayed into an area where great philosophers and theologians have foundered, and where inept phrasing is a constant menace, for the resources of language are too scant to express, at one and the same time, the fullness of grace and the amplitude of freedom, the reality of uncreated eternity, and the reality of chronological time, as well as its uncertainty.

Thérèse quite properly realizes that here she is dealing with "things that thought can scarcely represent, and things so deep that they reside only in the innermost recesses of the soul."

Out of the mouths of babes and sucklings. . . . Unwittingly, like another, though more orthodox Calvin, she consigns the soul to the refuge of merciful predestination, where love conquers all fear, and there is no trace of the anguish and dread that usually accompany that concept.

*   *   *

Accordingly, once she returns to the less exalted realms of time present, she is able to say that this moment now, which she seems at the same time to declare is illusory, is almost infinitely worthwhile.

I have already remarked, if in other terms, that one of the most profound and subtle of all the problems that the mind can wrestle with is that of shifting from eternity into time, and from time into eternity. Most of the great mystics try to resolve it by the also profound but erroneous (one might say profoundly erroneous) observation that salvation is not something to be sought when time is at an end, in an eternity of blessedness "beginning" then, but that we enter eternal life when, like the greatest artists, we experience certain moments of eternity. Some moments of perfect joy, so it is said, are equal to eternity, and even eternity itself: "Shall my sense pierce love,—the last relay / And ultimate outpost of eternity?" (Rossetti).

According to some pundits of the existential and similar schools of thought, the ethical sense, or the knowledge and practice of morality to the highest degree, can often afford moments of perfect joy which are virtually moments of eternity. Such occasions are so intense, it is said, that you are dispensed even from the need to hope, for they allow you to feel, but on earth, that you do indeed possess some share in eternity. In fact, there are some very elevated forms of argument (usually philosophical) about ethical intensity, and some extremely subtle expositions of what it means to hold "Infinity in the palm of your hand, and Eternity in an hour." They are found as far back as Aristotle. Spinoza ("By eternity I understand existence itself . . ."), and even Jean-Jacques Rousseau and Jean-Paul Sartre afford good examples. Of course there are also some degraded and vulgar forms of this line of argument. All apologies for the pleasure of the senses, for example, consist of promising infinite happiness in the present.

The error of even the most refined versions of these doctrines is not to suppose that the present moment is the only point at which humanity can communicate with the absolute, nor to suggest that the present moment, the essence of the here-and-now, can be tantamount to the sacrament of eternity in time. The metaphysical error here consists on the one hand of asserting that the present moment, which is temporal and earthbound, can be the equivalent of eternal beatitude, and on the other hand of necessarily denying the existence and condemning the hope of eternity after death, and doing so precisely in order to elevate a desire for the "eternity" of particular earthbound moments to a position of such total supremacy that it becomes the only possible eternity. To all intents and purposes, when taken to its logical conclusion in respect of the ultimate use and point of time, and hope in a hereafter, this idea is a practical definition of atheism. "Eat, drink and be merry, for tomorrow we die." St Paul cites this motto of carnal man, with its then logical denial of the future, let alone the future life. One of St Thomas Aquinas' most profound remarks was that the fruit of lust is the horror of the age to come: *Odium futuri saeculi.* "After me the deluge." Such is the philosophic error of an approach that advocates the following as a rule of conduct: "Choose the perfect moments and cheat time of its power! This will be our only eternity and sole salvation."

But the almost inevitable consequence, fruit, and in a sense punishment of this spiritual error is that this elevation of the search for, and of the enjoyment of, the purest moments of intellectual or artistic contemplation gives way to a celebration of mediocre moments of feeling and ultimately to a concentration on mere flashes of sensual pleasure—which is the sole religion of a great number of people.

Moreover, the really difficult aspect of all this is, as Bossuet says, to keep hold on both ends of the chain: both to see time as mere transience, that is "as nothing," and to think of the present instant as the only place where salvation and joy may be found, that is, as "everything."

Cardinal Mercier, a great admirer of Thérèse, said: "In the end, we have to ask what all that long interplay of secondary causes in our past life whose strings were held by Providence really amounts to. Could it all have been just a preparation for the present moment? Then I no longer have to worry about the past, which no longer exists, or to be anxious about the future, which has not yet happened. Let me consecrate myself to the present moment and nothing else, and then—though with the rapid heart-beats of ultimate apprehension and tense awareness of what it involves—act fearlessly and bring it to fruition."

We can find the same thoughts in Thérèse's work, though she puts it more poetically, of course. Her canticle is a good example:

My life is but an instant, a mere passing hour,
My life escapes and flies away, this single day, no
    other.
You know, O Lord: To love you on this earth,
I have this day, no other! . . .

What matters, Lord, a future bleak?
Beg you for tomorrow, I shall not, cannot! . . .
But keep my heart pure, put me in your shade
Just for this day, no other.

Soon I shall fly to sing your praise,
And leave this day, no other.
Then I shall play the angels' lyre,
And no longer say that on my soul it sets,
This day, no other,

But on my soul it shines:
Your everlasting day, all other! . . .

I have often been struck by the similarity between the spirituality of St Thérèse of the Child Jesus and that of Fr Jean-
Pierre de Caussade (1675-1751). His spiritual classic *Self-
Abandonment to Divine Providence* was extraordinarily successful when it was first published, in Paris in 1861. A Jesuit,
Fr Ramière, had skillfully put it together by using extracts
from de Caussade's letters. It was reprinted throughout the
nineteenth century and well into the twentieth. De Caussade
had a kind of genius; all those for whom the book has been a
constant companion will bear witness to this. In his work he
may be said to have reconciled the valuable, indeed superb,
yet antithetical French spiritual writers of the seventeenth
century, Bossuet and Fénelon, even though he did not have
their talent. He possessed neither the correct but dry doctrine
of the one, nor the flexibility and slightly equivocal gentleness
of the other, but his writing has assurance, acuity, and simple
wisdom, and exhibits an occasional astonishing virtuosity of

language. How, then, is he like Thérèse? Most probably in his development of the idea that abandonment is a general disposition you either acquire or are born with, as it were, but the due exercise of which demands an acceptance of God's will as to what you actually abandon yourself to. God's will is summed up in the quality of the present moment, which becomes an abridgement of divine providence and thus penetrates our mental and spiritual faculties, and consequently the things we apprehend or act upon. For de Caussade, it is all a matter of enjoying or not enjoying God. Enjoying God means loving him with a "pure love" full of confidence and light. Not enjoying him is pure faith, though in darkness, yet the shadows of this night are all pure, for "pure love sees, feels and believes, whereas pure faith believes without seeing or feeling." De Caussade expresses very well that perfect, deep, and pure identity of each and every thing with everything—an identiy that results from one and the same divine action both filling the infinite spaces of infinity and reducing them, so to speak, to the infinitely small compass of each human second.

There are also similarities between Thérèse from Normandy and a forerunner of hers, the Abbé de Touraille, who lived at the end of the last century and was a contemporary of Thérèse's (without knowing anything about her). There is no overall study of this spiritual thinker and, in so many ways, innovative philosopher. One is needed to show the connections between his thinking on social action (in the tradition of Le Play) and spirituality. He was a pupil of the best spiritual directors of the nineteenth century, in particular Mgr Gay and Mgr de Ségur. His contacts with the English-speaking world and his active life (which was also full of suffering), gave him an added dimension and up-to-date viewpoints, and a degree of certainty, audacity and joy unusual in the French school of spirituality, which is still characteristically austere. De Touraille's approach is very much like that of de Caussade, though there is less emphasis on metaphysics, and less sublimity. At the same time, he remains more amenable for the generality of people in a way that anticipates Thérèse's even more sympathetic mixture of simplicity and joy.

As de Touraille says:

> It is absolutely necessary to make your present life a happy one and to allow the grace you are granted now all its beneficent potential. You must turn this present grace into something good and much more intense yet also more normal and natural than you or anyone else ever imagined it could be.
>
> God is full of loving indulgence for those who value it, which means that he gives them latitude, not to offend him but to love him with a more trusting and confident heart, a more liberated and open attitude and a more passionate spirit.

Thérèse, Edith, Elizabeth

As I mentioned at the beginning of this book, another very relevant, if at first seemingly improbable, figure for comparison with Thérèse, is Bd Edith Stein (1891-1942), in religion Sr Benedicta of the Cross. She was a Carmelite philosopher and theologian, a Jewish convert, and a disciple of the German philosopher Husserl. After reading the life of St Teresa of Avila, she was baptized, became a Carmelite nun, but left Germany during the Nazi dictatorship to protect her Sisters there from persecution. She sought refuge in a Carmelite house in the Netherlands, determined to share the suffering of Christ. Her Jewish ancestry made her a victim of the barbaric anti-Semitic laws applied during the German occupation. She was transported in a cattle-truck to the German extermination camp at Auschwitz in Poland and murdered in the gas chambers there merely because she was a member of Christ's own people and born in the same faith (see the biography by Hilda Graef for a full account). Edith Stein's character was somewhat different from that of Thérèse Martin. She had the unflinching devotion to truth and a noble refusal to bow to any conviction other than that of conscience associated with the great tradition of Jewish spirituality. Her intensely philosophic cast of mind and unshakeable assurance of belief were utterly sincere yet without the more immediately joyful simplicity we associate with Thérèse. She did not come from that small-minded community, rooted in the soil, which formed the backbone of France. Instead she belonged to a Jewish family transiently resident in eastern Europe but living in continual fear of persecution and forced flight. Her vocation was a wholehearted commitment, not only to the idea that so possessed her, but to the unremitting precision of the structure and unrelenting, all-possessing idealism of the idea itself.

She was absolutely devoted to her teacher, Husserl, the founder of "phenomenology," whose intellectual methodology, rather than actual ideas, had a Thomist background. She grew out of phenomenology and veered more toward a revised form of Thomism, just as she had moved on through Judaism to arrive at Catholicism, and from baptism to the point of entering Carmel.

In spite of this involved intellectual and ideological background, and her tragic martyrdom under a despicable tyranny, there are profound similarities between the two Carmelites.

They both insisted on the simplicity of love. A friend of Edith's wrote to say that when she read Thérèse's *The Story of a Soul*, she was quite put off by its vapidity. Edith, the philosopher, replied: "I am surprised to read your reaction to little Thérèse. Until now, I never even dreamed that anyone could find her insipid. My impression was one of coming face-to-face with someone totally penetrated by the love of God, to the uttermost depths of her being. I do not know of anything greater, and it is some small part of that that I long, to whatever extent I may be granted it, to have in my own life and to introduce into the lives of everyone around me." The two nuns, Edith and Thérèse, show the same unremitting devotion to and longing for truth. "Everything about her is absolutely true," Husserl said of Edith Stein. And also: "How remarkable to see Edith discover, as if from a mountain top, the clarity and breadth of the horizon with such wonderful nimbleness of mind and purity of endeavour." Dom Walzer wrote: "She and I firmly believed that an untrammelled form of devotion was best. She was utterly uncomplicated."

Elisabeth de Miribel has produced some perceptive essays on Edith Stein, which suggest a number of other similarities between the two nuns and reveal them as sisters in religious disposition and basic inclination in spite of very different, indeed quite contrary, outward circumstances.

Their family relationships, for instance, are quite revealing in this respect. Thérèse was very deeply devoted to her very Catholic father who, toward the end of his life, became very ill and almost lost his mind altogether. Edith had an equal love for her Jewish mother, who never converted to Catholicism. Yet the members of Thérèse's family were totally sympathetic and understanding toward little Thérèse. Edith, however, was alone and misunderstood.

Whereas Thérèse had read little and was almost uneducated, Edith had read everything, especially in modern philosophy and mystical theology. She had been a university professor and a contributory participant in congresses on phenomenology. She wrote an extremely dense work on *The Finite and the Infinite*.

Thérèse died after a long illness, but in a white bed, surrounded by her sisters, and in the peace of the infirmary. Edith died an unimaginably lonely death, without sisters or companions, in the choking poison gas of Auschwitz, and her body was thrown like rubbish into an incinerator oven.

But, however different their situations were, even in death, they came to terms with them in very similar ways. It is as if their joint message to us was that the quality of love is all that really matters, whatever the circumstances. Pascal said: "Treat the big things as small because Jesus is sovereign, and the small things as big, because he is all-powerful."

Bd Elizabeth of the Trinity (1880-1906), or Elizabeth Catez from Dijon, was a very different figure to Edith Stein. The circumstances of her life are more akin to those of Thérèse's, but she did not leave an impressive body of writing to make her personality live for us in the same way. She was a discalced Carmelite and had a similarly short life; she also suffered constant ill health with immense courage. Above all, she is remembered for what that quiet mystic, Brother Lawrence, called the "practice of the presence of God." It is her profound awareness of the constancy and love of God that makes her so like Thérèse.

All three Carmelites are henceforth companions for us in what is most essential: Thérèse of Lisieux; Elizabeth of the Trinity from Dijon; and Edith Stein from Breslau (then Germany, now Wroclaw in Poland). One might even say that as one moves eastward, the intellect becomes more developed. Elizabeth of the Trinity is better educated than Thérèse; Edith towers over Elizabeth with her learning. For me, this brings out the essential subject of this book all the more clearly, as in its title, where for want of a better word I have used "genius" (*ingenium*) to describe something completely new, more direct, more revivifying, yet something unutterably simple, more communicable, more sympathetic to people in general and to the humble, something much less specific and learned, and more imitable by sinners, that what people generally mean by genius rather than the superlatively trained intellect. "That only is true enlargement of mind," says Newman,

> which is the power of viewing many things at once as one whole, of referring them generally to their true place in the universal system, of understanding their respective values, and determining their mutual dependence. . . . To have even a portion of this illuminative reason and true philosophy is the highest state to which nature can aspire, in the way of intellect; it puts the mind above the influences of chance and necessity, above anxiety, suspense, unsettlement, and superstition, which is the lot of the many. . . . [Then] there are men who, when in difficulties, originate at the moment vast ideas or dazzling projects; who, under the influence of excitement, are able to cast a light, almost as if from inspiration, on a subject or course of action which comes before them; who have a sudden presence of mind equal to any emergency, rising with the occasion, and an undaunted magnanimous bearing, and an energy and keenness which is but made intense by opposition. This is genius, this heroism; it is the exhibition of a natural gift which no culture can teach, at which

no Institution can aim. . . . [Yet] that perfection of the Intellect, which is the result of Education, and its beau ideal, to be imparted to individuals in their respective measures, is the clear, calm, accurate vision and comprehension of all things, as far as the finite mind can embrace them, each in its own place, and with its own characteristics upon it . . . it has almost the beauty and harmony of heavenly contemplation, so intimate is it with the eternal order of things and the music of the spheres. (*The Idea of a University*, pp. 138-9)

But, as if to reassure us, he also says: "Innocence, simplicity, implicit obedience to God, tranquillity of mind, contentment, these and the like virtues are themselves a sort of wisdom;—I mean, they produce the same results as wisdom, because God works for those who do not work for themselves . . . it is the power of Divine grace, their state of heart." (*Sermons bearing upon Subjects of the Day*, pp. 299-300)

Newman often refers to this particular quality of genius as the highest of gifts. It is the instinctive possession of intuitive knowledge produced neither by the superlative exercise of reason nor by investigation. And those who use their intuition to communicate with moral truth reach, in the spiritual part of their nature, that rare spiritual perfection which he rightly calls "one of the intellectual properties of the soul."

Thérèse's Devotion to Mary

Traditionally, the Carmelite Order is dedicated to the Virgin Mary, whom it looks on as exercising sovereignty over all worlds, or realms visible and invisible, including purgatory. This is certainly what is tacitly implied by the terms of the consecration and devotion of all members of the Order to Our Lady handed down from the time of Simon Stock, the Englishman (and commemorated as a saint, though never formally canonized) who became sixth general of the Order (*c.* 1247). He was said to have been honoured with an extraordinary privilege by Mary, who appeared to him in a vision, holding the scapular of the Order in her hand, and saying: "This will be a privilege for you and for all Carmelites. Anyone who dies in this habit will be saved."

Admittedly, most of the great religious Orders are favoured by Our Lady's special protection, or at least have a particular way of showing it. Mary reigns over each of these Orders, like light reflected from a multi-facetted diamond. It is as if she bestowed on each facet a ray of sunlight which was then refracted and reflected in a unique way, reaching eventually each individual with the quality peculiar to that facet which he or she could reflect personally, while relying both on the facet and the original source of light. But, in a certain very daring sense, the Carmelites also lay claim to an even more remote tradition which dates back to antiquity, as it were, and which derives from a much older dispensation. In this understanding, it is as if the Carmelites had been founded even before Jesus Christ himself, by the Virgin Mary in an earlier manifestation; by, that is to say, the very Idea of the Virgin as she already existed in God himself.

The Carmelite Order does not find it necessary even to refer to Our Lady, to use any of her titles, or specifically to promote and elevate any one of her attributes. Instead, the very ethos, the atmosphere, of the Carmelite Order is Marian. In its foundation, consecration, and rule of silence, it is impregnated with the very idea of Mary. Similarly, the life of any branch of the Order, and the life of any individual Carmelite, even if it does not formally recommend and precisely delineate or follow any special imitation of Mary, is essentially imbued with and breathes the spirit of Mary as something understood, so to speak, from all eternity. It is infused from before the start with what one might call a Marian potentiality, which then becomes interfused with the potentiality proper to humanity and the individual self.

This makes any analytical approach to the subject more difficult, because nowadays what we call analysis is associated with what can be formulated rationally and stated empirically, and with whatever can be broken down into ascertainable constituent elements. Certainly, the (now scarcely novel) twentieth-century method of analysis of the psyche, or mind-and-soul, known formerly as depth psychology but now generally known as psychoanalysis, still claims to be able by various strategies to detect, scrutinize, and reveal the deepest structures of the unconscious self. But, even nowadays, neither that approach nor many others with similar and analogous claims can elicit and define a human being's true essence and potentiality: the potential which is an essential aspect of humanity from the moment of conception, even from the time of a pre-existent shadowy sense of what will come to be, but certainly as it exists in the depths of this or that person now, already heralding what he or she will be in the future.

It is necessary to draw attention to this difficult yet essential truth on the threshold of this particular phase of my study of Thérèse's personality and approach. This profound law of potentiality in all existence, and undoubtedly of all Carmelite life in the form of the Marian ethos traditionally and mystically proper to it, governed the life of Thérèse of the Child

Jesus too. We cannot expect, then, to encounter the Virgin Mary throughout Thérèse's life and piety in the sense of the familiar devotional figure, constantly manifest and referred to in traditional imagery and language, even in anything like the practice of many of the foremost mystics of the French school of spirituality who have been rediscovered in the second half of the twentieth century (I am thinking here especially of M. Ollier, Bérulle, St Jean Eudes, and specially of St Louis-Marie Grignion de Montfort). They have a certain relevance to Thérèse, to be sure, but in a somewhat different context.

Many admirable studies have appeared of the more commonplace aspects of Thérèse's Marian piety (the most outstanding of which, in my opinion, are those by Henri Martin, Fr Combes, Fr Victor of the Virgin, and Fr Nicolas). I shall try neither to reproduce nor to plagiarize them. Instead I shall avoid well-trodden paths, and offer a few impressions which, though personal, are perhaps fresh enough to complement received ideas on the subject.

Certainly, in a traditionally Christian family like Thérèse's, she would have been brought up from a very early age with a special devotion to Our Lady. Yet, even then, in the way proper to those whom one might call original spirits of the "angelic" type, she made everything she said seem fresh and novel. Even when using conventional expressions and traditional phraseology, she was able to revivify them with an additional intensity. To grow in spiritual life is to simplify matters. It also means simplifying oneself in order to approach and come closer to the uncreated and indescribable simplicity of God. This does not imply anything like that false kind of simplification which necessarily impoverishes an idea, when one tries to make plain what would otherwise prove obfuscating (as when an adult tries to describe a mystery to a child). True simplification should enrich and add quality to a concept, so that it becomes an immediately meaningful call-sign for its true sublimity. Accordingly, a "spiritual childhood" is not the first but the last phase of the spiritual life, even though some people (who still have to make an unusual effort to do so) are granted the extraordinary privilege of reaching this stage when they are scarely more than children themselves.

I have selected from the notes I took on my reading, without reference to date or chronological order, some of the things that Thérèse actually wrote about the Virgin Mary. I have chosen three particular passages and points for emphasis, in full awareness that they and others could be presented more systematically in the framework of a comparative study beyond the scope of the present work. However paradoxical this may seem, I hope that my concentration on the hidden virtue of what have hitherto been thought of as minor aspects of Thérèse's devotion to Mary will help to bring out essential points overlooked by other commentators and even, perhaps, by Thérèse herself. These obscure areas can often shed light on what is most hidden within a human being, and yield insights into a personality that will allow an authentic form of "psychoanalysis" to be carried out "in spirit and in truth."

In her autobiography, of course, Thérèse remembers making wreaths of daisies and forget-me-nots for Our Lady's statue during the month of May, and also describes the "little white book case, with my lesson-books and note-books on it; that also had to hold a statue of Our Lady, with fresh flowers in vases, and some candles round it; let alone a quantity of other holy statues." Then there is the famous "wonder-working statue of the Madonna which had twice given Mother the Message she needed." Toward this statue, Thérèse says, she would "turn continually, like a flower that turns its head toward the sun." When she, Thérèse, was very ill, her father paid for a novena of Masses to be said in Paris in honour of Our Lady of Victories. Then, one Sunday in the course of Thérèse's five weeks of pain and delirious phases, Marie and her other sisters turned toward this statue and prayed for their sister, and Thérèse turned toward it too:

> . . . and all my heart went out into a prayer that my Mother
> in Heaven would have pity on me. All at once, she let me
> see her in her beauty, a beauty that surpassed all my experi-
> ence—her face wore such a look of kindness and of pity as
> I can't describe; but what pierced me to the heart was her
> smile, "that entrancing smile of the Blessed Virgin's."
> With that, all my distress came to an end . . . And I said to
> myself: "To think that the Blessed Virgin should have
> smiled down at me! Oh, I'm so happy! But I mustn't tell
> anyone about it; my happiness would disappear if I did."

She remarks that it was to Marie she owed "this privilege of a
smile from the Queen of Heaven herself." Of course, having in
the end told Marie about her belief that the Virgin had been
especially gracious to her, Thérèse had certain scruples about
this event: "For four years the memory of that wonderful grace
I'd received was a real torment to me, and when I found happiness again, it was only at the feet of Our Lady of Victories."
When the nuns at Carmel heard about it and questioned her
("Was the Blessed Virgin carrying the Child Jesus in her arms?
Was there a great blaze of light . . . ?"), "These questions
worried me and made me feel unhappy; I could only go on
saying: 'The Blessed Virgin looked very beautiful indeed and I
saw her smile down at me.' After all, it was only her face,
really, that had caught my attention; and here were these
Carmelites getting the whole thing wrong!" In spite of these
remarks, Thérèse's account of the incident is so ambiguously
composed that it remains uncertain whether she refers throughout to the statue itself, or also to a conviction that Mary had
actually appeared to her for a moment and smiled at her.

Then there is the occasion when Thérèse recited her act of
consecration to Our Lady on the afternoon of her first Communion day: ". . . it was only fair that I, who had lost my
earthly mother so young, should talk to my heavenly Mother
in the name of the rest. . . . I think she smiled down at me

from heaven, unseen; hadn't she smiled down visibly at me, and given life to the little flower that seemed to be fading away? And now she had brought her own Son to birth in me, the wild rose on the lowland plain, the wild lily on the mountain slopes."

Other poems and declarations to Our Lady, such as the verses of "Why I love you, O Mary," summarizing her experience of devotion to Our Lady, in the very twilight of her short life (PN 54), were among the many ways in which she carried out each intention listed in the act of consecration she made in the abbey on May 31, 1887:

> O Mary, conceived without sin,
> I, Marie Françoise Thérèse Martin, . . .
>
> I declare that henceforth
> I shall belong to you without reservation,
> I shall walk in your glorious footsteps
> And imitate your virtues,
> Especially your angelic purity,
> Your blind obedience
> And your incomparable charity.

For those new to the details of Thérèse's life, I merely record these occasions as part of the background necessary to grasp the full important of subsequent remarks, but avoid any lengthy comment on what is largely self-explanatory. I want to concentrate on the three passages that follow.

1. THE COMMON WAY AND FAITH PURE AND SIMPLE

How I love her, the Virgin Mary! How I would have liked to have been a priest so that I could preach about her! We are taught that she is inaccessible, but we should be told that she can be imitated. She is more a Mother than a Queen! I have heard it said that, because of her privileges, she eclipses all the saints, just as the rising sun makes the stars disappear! Well, I think the exact opposite. I believe that she greatly increases the splendour of the souls in heaven. . . . The Virgin Mary! How simple I think her life must have been!" (Summary version of DE 21.8.3.)

As always, Thérèse's thoughts here are very daring. She stresses the idea that Mary lived an ordinary, workaday life. There is no reference to wonder-working. From the age of fourteen, Thérèse had an intuitive conviction (amazing in one so young) that miracles are appropriate to those of slight or wavering faith, whom they strengthen and confirm in it. But for those close to him, particularly in his mother's case, "Jesus did not perform miracles, before testing their faith." For Thérèse, Mary's was a life of faith pure and simple, of faith unqualified.

This belief made her unwilling to exaggerate anything in the life of, or her own devotion to, Our Lady. Her certain preference in exegetical writing, as shown in her own work when it may at all be characterized thus, is for restraint rather than excess. When writing on Our Lady in the past, I have always taken as my maxim (though without any explicit reference to Thérèse) this passage from the *Novissima*: "It is not necessary to say incredible things about her or things that cannot be known. For a sermon on the Holy Virgin to please and inspire me, I have to contemplate her REAL and not her supposed life."

In the Virgin Mary, Thérèse admired a strong faith which believes without seeing and persists through all darkness. She probably accepted her trials as an unimportant person in a somewhat retrograde world, but also, as she entered the empty valley of its shadow, the prospect of her own death, because she could imitate what she thought of as Mary's own trials. Or, more precisely:

In the second phase of her life, Thérèse would seem to have given up any expectation of a visible manifestation of Mary's help, in the sense of anything like the ecstatic "smile" and "miracle" she had attributed to Our Lady of Victories, and of course the somewhat irritating outcome of that incident. An all but overriding conviction became increasingly evident: namely, the idea that she should let nothing out of the ordinary, let alone "supernatural," be seen in her approach and life, so that everything about her would be imitable by everyone. That is why Thérèse insisted on the ordinariness of the Virgin Mary, which could be imitated by everyone. But that, of course, is exactly what St Luke also had in mind.

For Thérèse, Mary's way of life and faith is devoid of ecstasy, miracles, and even words. The Virgin, Thérèse noted, "marvelled at" the prophecies which the venerable Simeon (the just and devout old man who had been told that he would not die until he had seen the Messiah) uttered about the baby Jesus when he took him in his arms. For Thérèse, Mary's attitude showed "a certain degree of surprise on her part." For Mary, as Thérèse saw her, and almost certainly for Thérèse herself, simple faith was allied with a certain kind of ignorance, of perplexity overcome with a heroic effort, and of battling on in a perpetual half-light.

Like Jean-Pierre de Caussade (along the lines of his recommendations in his famous *Self-Abandonment to Divine Providence*, which I am sure she owned or at least had read to the extent that she lived and breathed its message), Thérèse must have believed that the most extraordinary thing is that there is actually nothing which can properly be termed extraordinary, and that faith offers us now, in this present moment, an overwhelming experience of Infinity: the "sacrament of the present moment." What we know of her is wholly in accord with the de Caussade who referred to each passing moment as both the veil of God and, when disclosed by faith, the unveiling of God; to Christian life as cooperating with God actively and passively moment by moment; and to prayer as simple openness to God, discerning his presence, and cooperating with him in the exercise of his will.

These tendencies are clear in Thérèse's writings. It is also evident what kind of Marian theology she would have preferred, if she had lived longer, and had read and studied more. She would surely have approved of those theologian psychologists who are intent on describing the development of Mary's awareness in a state of intermittent lack of secure knowledge, in the tradition of Newman. She would not have been surprised to read, as in some of Fr de Broglie's lectures, for example, that Mary did not see things clearly, but must have had to accept and believe much as we do. Perhaps she would have acknowledged the view of some mystics, that the reason why the risen Jesus did not appear to his mother was because she did not need this particular sign and because her faith remained totally pure. At any rate, Thérèse would have been happy to know that certain modern spiritual thinkers in the mid-twentieth century had arrived at a much more humanly responsible understanding of the purifying effect of the trials of faith and its implications, of the moments of desertion and absence, of the "abandonment to divine providence," to which Jesus may be said to have subjected his mother as the exemplary human vehicle of God's holy Word.

At the same time, we know that Thérèse did not accept simplistic statements that Our Lady, after hearing Simeon's prophecy (namely, that "This child is destined for the falling and the rising of many in Israel, and to be a sign that will be opposed so that the inner thoughts of many will be revealed— and a sword will pierce your own soul too" [Luke 2. 34-5]), had had to go on living, as it were, in full consciousness of a future suffering which she therefore continually experienced. On the contrary, Thérèse thought that because Mary did not know at what point in the future whatever might happen would happen, her "blind"—or, rather, pure and simple— faith in fact allowed her fully to accept the sacrament of the present moment: the joy or difficulties of each God-willed moment of her life.

2. OUR LADY AND THE EUCHARIST

We discover a second, rather novel, aspect of Thérèse's devotion to Mary in the associations which she discerned between the Virgin and the Eucharist. Henri Martin makes an intelligent point in this respect. He notes that when Thérèse received communion she did so in union with Mary. She did this as a means not only of self-purification or self-preparation but of asking Our Lady to get rid of the "ruins," of everything dead, worn-out and useless, and erect a vast tent or tabernacle within her, Thérèse, adorned with all the precious things that would make it worthy of heaven:

> Change my heart, Virgin Mary.
> Into a pure and beautiful Corporal. . . .
>
> (PN 25, 4)

She expressed the same idea but with greater force in her last poem:

> When the white Host comes down into my heart,
> Jesus, your Gentle Lamb believes it is resting
> in you! . . .
>
> (PN 54, 5)

The subtle thinking behind this imagery is related to the theme of substitution, which, in one way or another, appears in the writings of many mystics. But there is certainly much more to Thérèse's metaphysical simile, which certainly includes much more than the foregoing and much more that is almost inexpressible in the language of literary analysis. As St Thomas Aquinas put it in his famous rhythmic "prose," now widely sung as a communion hymn:

> AVE VERUM CORPUS NATUM DE MARIA
>   VIRGINE
> Hail, true Body, born of Mary,
> Spotless Virgin's virgin birth;
> Thou who truly hangedst weary

> On the Cross for sons of earth;
> Thou whose sacred side was riven,
> Whence the Water flowed and Blood,
> O may'st thou, dear Lord, be given
> At death's hour to be my food:
> O most kind! O gracious One!
> O sweetest Jesu, holy Mary's Son!

An important aspect of what St Thomas is saying here is that, contrary to the Docetists or the Monophysites, the *corpus mysticum*, the mystical Body of the Eucharist, is the very same one that was born of Mary in human history, and through her of the whole preceding human race. In a poem of somewhat questionable taste, which would lead modern psychoanalytical critics into byways of profitless speculation, Thérèse tried to express the relationship between Mary's virginity and the integrity—the wholeness or oneness—of *corpus Christi*, the body of Christ:

> The Bread of Angels is the Virgin's Milk (PN 1).

This topic was so dear to Thérèse that she asked Céline to paint a picture on the theme. She kept the rather syrupy result in her breviary.

Thérèse and Céline were inspired by St Augustine (with Mary of St Peter, a Carmelite from Tours, and Fr Louis d'Argentan, a Capucin monk, as intermediaries). The following text was a particular favourite: "It was necessary that the divine substance should pass through Mary's breast to become a milk appropriate to our childhood weaknesses:" in short, the "sincere milk of the word," the *lac rationabile, logikon gala*, which St Peter says that we, as newborn babes, should desire (1 Pet. 2:2).

There are similar remarks in the writings of St Francis de Sales and Grignion de Montfort, but (as far as I am aware) it is only grace, and not the Eucharist, which they compare with "divine milk." These great spiritual writers do not go so far as our extremely daring Child Thérèse, in turning *panis angelicus* and *lac virginale*, manna and Mary's milk, into a single metaphor.

Perhaps Thérèse would have preferred silence to a translation of these and her irreducible intuitions into the terminology of our now more mundane language. Yet here we are evidently faced with one of her deep-rooted and very personal themes, without a definable source in any particular book. Of course, when her sister Céline, who did not possess Thérèse's genius but took the main lines of her thought and practice from her, became Sister Geneviève, and designed her own sacred "coat of arms," it included the Virgin's monogram intertwined with grapes and thorns.

3. SUBSTITUTING SITUATIONS

"Oh Mary, if I were the Queen of Heaven and you were Thérèse, I would change places with Thérèse so that you could be Queen of Heaven!!!" (Pr. 21).

These were the last lines that Thérèse wrote.

Thérèse called this thought a childish fancy, perhaps because it was a very old idea of hers and it recalled vague childhood intuitions. Sometimes a child's words are unfathomable; at a very early age, the human consciousness is unaware of the exact import, or effect, of what is passing through a child's lips, for the child-mind is incapable of the hard, slow, crystal-clear, but often immensely subtle, and even Mephistophelean, process of "reflection." It is possible to make sense of Thérèse's "childish fancy" if we make a distinction between objective and subjective beauty.

Beauty is a form of splendour which should be capable of appreciation quite apart from its possessor, without his or her awareness of its existence, or he or she taking it into account when thinking about himself or herself.

Beauty is a kind of additional aspect of being that shines out from the person who is nevertheless distinct from it. We might say that the person who is beautiful, or who tells the truth, or who talks of things to do with God, should neither know that he or she emanates that beauty, or tells that truth, or talks thus, nor take pleasure in being or doing so. Then it is not the objective possessor of beauty who truly possesses it, unless he or she, like Narcissus, selfishly contemplates himself or herself in a mirror: it is the other.

We might say that the most enviable situation is not to be the subject of beauty and to know that one is beautiful, but to be the object of beauty, so that the other alone takes pleasure in what emanates from you.

Let us imagine a person of such clarity and perfect humility that he or she never contemplates the beauty of his or her own soul or body, or merit, and possesses all these gifts without knowing it, and above all without having them. Such an individual will ignore himself or herself totally and will be reduced to a state of perfect simplicity.

In one sense, the position of an onlooker would be more privileged than that of the person endowed with beauty, for the person contemplating it from without would enjoy that beauty, whereas the beautiful person himself or herself would not.

Accordingly, I can see a primary (though very difficult) meaning in this childhood observation. It is better to be Thérèse than Thérèse's queen, for the queen does not see herself as a queen. She is queen above all in the heart of the one who contemplates her.

Mary's beauty becomes startingly apparent in people who see Mary as she is, because her extraordinary humility and the absolute perfection of the way in which she is perfectly joined to God is a profoundly beautiful situation in which giving and being given are mysteriously one and the same; in other words, Mary's beauty is not something to be baldly contemplated and enjoyed in anything like the ordinary human sense of possessing and taking pleasure. In a way, Mary is no longer Mary on her own, Mary herself, but Mary taken up into God her

Saviour, in whom, although she is still Mary, she finds fulfilment. She has entered the complex of everlasting love. Moreover, she has entered it in such a way that we poor ordinary human beings who are fortunate enough to know her have, dare we say, an advantage compared with her. This is something that a portrait painter would readily understand, for he or she sees the model in a way in which that person would never be able properly to see and understand himself or herself.

* * *

There is a second meaning to Thérèse's "childlike" yet sublime idea—one that relies on the aspect not of knowledge but of charity.

If Thérèse were queen and the Virgin Mary only a servant, love would compel Thérèse to exchange places and roles; for there is more glory at the summit than in obscurity, more joy in giving than in receiving. Thérèse as queen would sacrifice everything, so that her servant could become queen and possess everything. This is the dialectic between having everything and having nothing about which the *Imitation of Christ* (a book so loved by Thérèse that she learnt it by heart, particularly the chapter "On the wonderful effect of divine love." Book III, ch. 5) says: *Dat omnia pro omnibus et habet omnia in omnibus.* "It gives all to everyone and it possesses all in everyone."

Essentially, Thérèse's "childish fancy" contains the same fundamental intuition as the famous "slavery" of Grignion de Montfort, to which the Carmelite tradition had become so hostile. He was a popular missionary and, between 1701 and 1703, while chaplain at a hospital at Poitiers, founded the Daughters of Wisdom, a Congregation for nursing the sick and educating poor children. In 1712 he established the Company of Mary, a Congregation of missionaries. He wrote a treatise on "The True Devotion to the Holy Virgin," which was lost and then rediscovered in 1842 and had a powerful influence on Catholic devotion. We know that the Paris Carmelites were opposed to the ideas in this respect of Philippe de Bérulle (1575-1629), a diplomatist, theologian, and reformer who was made a cardinal in 1627. He was celebrated for his spiritual teaching, which showed such devotion to Christ as God-made-man that Urban VIII called him the "apostle of the Word incarnate." He imposed on the French Carmelites the "vow of servitude to Jesus and Mary" that Grignion de Montfort reinstated a century later.

The writings of Montfort, a Pindaric and Pauline genius, recall the approach, in both thought and style, of the metaphysical poets who preceded Socrates and whom the early twentieth century rediscovered after Nietzsche (1844-1900). He was of the same lyrical yet philosophical stock as the German mystical poets Angelus Silesius (1614-77), Novalis (1772-1801), and Friedrich Hölderlin (1770-1843). Essentially, however, in spite of these elevated associations, there is no more in Grignion de Montfort than we can find in the last text Thérèse wrote, in a very mysterious "childlike" adage. After all, the idea of giving everything in order to possess everything is the secret and, so to speak, the essential "process" of all absolutely radical love.

In spite of all these marginal and incomplete observations, it is true that St Thérèse most often speaks directly to Christ. Jesus appears as the primary and unique objective of her love and will to love, both in her more theoretical or doctrinal statements and in her everyday life. The thought of Mary remains, but remains implicit, in her first two manuscripts. For example, Thérèse does not mention Mary in the canticle of love which she composed in September 1896, even though that is a piece in which one might certainly expect to find Our Lady, for Thérèse wrote it especially for her sister Marie.

Here I should like to interpolate a more personal comment, based on my own experience and conviction, though of course I am aware that it may not be universally acceptable without a lengthy exposition. Devotion (by which I mean faith incarnated in a unique nature in accordance with the structure and traits of a particular temperament), much more than faith itself, accommodates a personal element that is natural, sensitive, and even "sexual," in the purest sense of the word. A son does not love his mother in the same way as a daughter loves the very same mother. From this viewpoint, that special element of a man's piety plays an essential part in devotion and in mysticism, especially for those who have taken vows of chastity and celibacy. A male religious who has decided not to exercise that aspect of nature in the usual ways finds a special kind of fulfilment in devotion to the Virgin Mary. Auguste Comte (1798-1857), the founder of French Positivism and of the "Religion of Humanity," and the foremost German poet, dramatist, and thinker, Johann Wolfgang von Goethe (1749-1832), neither of them a Catholic and scarcely a Christian or believer in any conventional sense, both noted this tendency in their very different works (one need think only of this theme as it recurs throughout Goethe's *Faust*, Parts I and II, but particularly in the final scenes of *Faust* II). Conversely, a woman may tend to approach Christ alone by a more vertical path, and in a sense an easier one, if you believe, as I do, that the feminine, much more than the masculine, heart is inclined to straightforward surrender.

At an even deeper level, however, we may say (together with the greatest spiritual thinkers and writers, the most pure of mystics, and the most inspired theologians) that devotion to Our Lady, in the very best sense, is the form directed to the Virgin Mother. Then it is wholly oriented toward Christ as God, and is essentially a direct path toward Him. Once separated from Christ, the Virgin Mary would be a pagan goddess. She derives her spiritual meaning and spiritual elevation from giving herself, whole and entire, to Christ who is God. And that is exactly how she appears from the viewpoint of St Thérèse of the Child Jesus.

In this respect, though not a theologian in the scholarly sense, Thérèse is one intuitively. Instinctively (and in accordance with the authentic Carmelite tradition), she drew on the greatest Masters: St John of the Cross as an introduction, then the Bible and above all the Gospels. Along those lines, Thérèse believes that if we were to contemplate Mary, and to love and be drawn to her as a created being, instead of contemplating her in her total oneness with God, seeing her in that way would produce an all too human form of affection. It would actually create an intermediary, and thus a barrier, between God and the individual soul and eventually lead it off in a variety of directions. One of Grignion de Montfort's profound ideas is that of Mary as the straight, direct and (so to speak) "immediating" way to God, a way that above all unifies and simplifies rather than diversifies and confuses. Pride is the constant principle of all false diversity and complication. In the mystical Marian spirituality of Maria a Sancta Theresia (Maria Petyt, 1623-77), a Carmelite tertiary, we find something approaching the same progress toward simplification, by way of a gradual exclusion of the mere external "Marian shell," which in the end is merely tacitly implied, leaving the soul alone with the divine Essence.

Thérèse followed the same pattern. Undoubtedly, from our knowledge of her particular cast of mind, she would have wholeheartedly and profoundly endorsed the writings on this subject of St John of the Cross, who avoided any too coarsely outward expression of his devotion to Our Lady. His piety in this respect was so intangible, delicate, and fragile, it seems, that had he put it into any too directly linguistic form· it would have evaporated like the most exquisitely perfect but evanescent perfume.

"Our Virgin Lady, all glorious within, being raised from the beginning to this high state of oneness, never had any creaturely form imprinted on her soul."

In his beautiful poem the *Spiritual Canticle*, and in his

extended commentaries on it, St John of the Cross offers us a dialogue of love in the course of which the soul, or Bride, is completely transformed in the Beloved:

> Why, when his arrows
> Have entered my heart,
> Is my life left dying
> From knowledge of him?
>
> For you were a robber
> Who left me for dead.
> Why not take with you
> The plunder you sought?
>
> Only for your sake
> Do I value my sight.
> Reveal yourself clearly
> And show me your face.

As the soul sees herself to be dying of love, and sees also that she is not dying wholly, in such a way as to be able to have fruition of love freely, she makes complaint of the duration of her bodily life, by reason of which her spiritual life is delayed. She addresses the very life of her soul, laying stress upon the pain which it causes her. Life of my soul, how can you persevere in this fleshly life, since it is death to you and privation of that true spiritual life of God, wherein in essence, love and desire you live more truly than in the body? And although this would be no cause for leaving and freeing yourself of the body of this death in order to enjoy and live the life of your God, how can you still persevere in the body so frail, since, besides this, the wound which you receive from the love of the grandeurs that are communicated to you from your Beloved are alone sufficient to end your life, all of which wounds leave you vehemently wounded with love; so that all the things which you feel and understand concerning him are so many touches and wounds which you receive, and which slay with love? . . . Besides many other different ways wherein God visits the soul, wounding it and upraising it in love, he is wont to bestow on it certain enkindling touches of love, which like fiery arrows strike and pierce the soul and leave it wholly cauterized with the fire of love. And these are properly called the wounds of love. So greatly do these wounds enkindle the will in affection that the soul finds itself burning in the fire and flame of love, so much so that it appears to be consumed in that flame which causes it to go forth from itself and be wholly renewed and enter upon another mode of being. . . . These visits he makes to wound the soul rather than to heal it, and to afflict rather than to satisfy, since they serve but to quicken the knowledge and increase the desire, and, consequently, the pain. These are called wounds of love, and are most delectable to the soul, for the which cause it would fain be ever dying a thousand deaths from these lance-thrusts, for they cause it to issue forth from itself and enter into God.

Although perfect love (John says) enables us to assess and understand painful and terrible things—that is, to apprehend their pain and terror—without actually suffering them, God sometimes does allow such perfect souls to feel and to suffer these trials. He permits this so that they may amass all the greater merit in a process which is then beneficial rather than destructive. This, of course, is precisely what happened in the case of Our Lady. For the same reason, Thérèse's devotion to Mary, as often happens for those who have an entirely pure and perfect apprehension of Our Lady's presence and nature, was almost entirely a matter of commitment to compassion pure and simple. In other words, it was a form of recourse to and concentration upon the heart of Mary the Immaculate, Our Lady of Sorrows. Purity and pain, after all, are inevitable companions.

One might summarize the foregoing by saying that, in the life of Thérèse of the Child Jesus, any explicit presence of Our

Lady takes second place to the presence of Jesus Christ as Thérèse finally leaves her childhood proper and enters the life of Carmel. Indeed, it is not going too far to say that Jesus' explicit humanity also—for want of a better term—takes second place to Thérèse's extraordinarily pure and mysterious faith and belief as she gets closer to the point of her own death. There is nothing daring, or inimical to absolute theological truth, in this assertion. A gradual process of this kind does not amount to some kind of erasure of the Divine. Instead it becomes a progress toward a meeting with pure essence: the mysterious ultimacy of God that can be approached only by following the way of the cross itself in total commitment to faith. This advance, which we find uniquely evident in Thérèse's adult life, is the pure way of the cross experienced in pure faith. It is a journey toward ultimate Purity undertaken in a state of purity.

In certain refined instances, authentic devotion to Mary may be said to become a form of address which, though always essentially human, is nevertheless devoid of certain aspects of "masculinity" and "femininity," though, of course, it does and must retain something of these basic qualities of being a human: the strength of love which is the essence of true masculinity, and that power of love which is the quintessence of real femininity. It would not be authentic devotion if it lacked the rigour and courage of the masculine aspect of humanity, or the divinely-inspired tenderness and surrender of its feminine side.

We must never forget that it was the rule and discipline of the Carmelite tradition that allowed all these best aspects of Thérèse's (Marian) piety and devotion (which we may call her essential purity of endeavour) a particular form and definition without which we could hardly sense, let alone appreciate, the private qualities of her personality and spirit.

Thérèse, Mary, and Protestantism

Consideration of Mary in Christian thinking is immensely important. Mary is not at the centre, because Christ is the only centre, but the place she does occupy gives her a vast ability, by inspiration and sympathy, to help Christian thought and practice on the way to its proper focus on Christ.

Catholicism, which is essentially concerned with the true spirit of universality and apostolic practice, typically rejoices at any signs that the Virgin Mary's role in bringing the family of faith together is duly acknowledged, that an understanding of her function is spreading, and that the real glory of the Saviour's mother is gradually becoming apparent in other denominations. Nevertheless, we have to recognize that almost any kind of development within Catholicism in the definition and understanding of Mary tends to alienate the churches of the Reformation from the Catholic Church. The separated churches of the Reformed tradition, which have certainly done much to maintain Christian tradition as it was when the various denominations were divided, tend to think of Marian piety and dogmas about the Virgin Mary as corruptions of the deposit of faith. Strange to say, Mary then becomes not the one before God who brings all her children together in his sight but the one who, in this way, seems to keep them divided.

A truly Catholic attitude to any proposition or definition that leads to greater understanding of the Virgin Mary should be one of greater joy and edification at a deeper understanding of the mysteries of God. Yet Catholics too sometimes find what should be so liberating is actually restrictive. It is not going too far to say that Mary herself must suffer in some way at seeing what is proposed as, and in one sense is, greater enlightenment increase the gulf between those of the same faith. To cite only one example, when Pope Pius XII was examining the advantages and disadvantages of defining the Assumption of Our Lady as a dogma of the Church (in 1950), he must have been torn between a desire to honour the Virgin and a very reasonable fear of placing yet another obstacle on the way to Christian union.

On this subject, as it concerns our thought about Thérèse, I find it most apposite to quote Fr Nicolas (writing some years ago in the French *Thomist Review*), whose approach is entirely in line with my own:

> In many respects, once all the merely local and unimportant references have been removed, Protestants must surely find the spirituality of Thérèse of Lisieux much less disconcerting than other forms of Catholic devotion and piety. Just think of her insistence on the fatherhood of God, her pure gospel spirit, her disinterested ethos of pure grace and of detachment from any thought of personal merit, her concern for the spirit rather than for the letter, her very daring criticism of many very off-putting and regrettable aspects of Catholic spirituality, her attraction for all sorts and conditions of people and even for those quite outside the religious life and the world of vows and promises. All this amounts to a major example of the very best values of the Reformation amazingly alive in Catholic spirituality itself. The way in which Thérèse approaches the mystery of Mary, and the image which she has and recommends of the Mother of God and her spirit, certainly seem more acceptable to Protestants than all those highly elaborate and high-sounding theological pronouncements which are justified by saying that they enable us to get to the bottom, and to tease out the profound, scholarly import, of what are actually very simple topics. A Protestant would really have little difficulty in understanding the most valuable aspects of Thérèse's thinking on Our Lady and devotion to her. Of course there are problems about the way in which she

expressed the relationship between her own innermost self and the Virgin Mary. For Thérèse, Our Lady was a very, very real person indeed. Her relationship with Mary, however direct and real, nevertheless took for granted a teaching which quite a number of Protestants find very suspect. Thérèse never doubted Mary's ability to mediate between us and Jesus, her role in the ways in which God's grace reaches us, and the part she plays in the inward life of human beings. Yet, in the end, any consistent and competent analysis of what Marian devotion really meant to Thérèse of Lisieux must help anyone to accept, or at least to understand, that it never reduces but actually preserves, whole and entire, the utterly pure, absolutely direct and entirely simple relationship between the human soul and God himself, who is the ultimate, sole true focus of the religious life and devotion of any human soul, whether Catholic, Protestant, or whatever. This is so, in spite of the major and, indeed, intimate place that Mary occupies in Thérèse's unique way of approaching God.

Seen in this light, Thérèse's Marian spirituality is an extremely fruitful basis for meditation and reflection. The spirit of Carmel in which it flourished actually tended to eradicate any exaggeration of, or undue excess in, devotion to Our Lady. In general, we may say (and this is entirely evident in the works of Grignion de Montfort) that the essential thrust of spirituality is directed toward simplification. In this, it is very like poetry and all great literature in which the lyrical impulse is predominant. It strives to reach the greatest possible degree of purity, just as science tries to achieve the nearest thing to ultimate integration. A spiritual thinker, writer, or practitioner in the best sense, whether he or she declares this to be the case or not, is engaged in producing what the eighteenth century above all thought of as a "short introduction," or "summary." Thomas à Kempis' *The Imitation of Christ*, for example, is an extraordinary essay in simplification compared with the over-the-top monastic devotion of that period, and indeed of many other times. The same is true of St Francis de Sales' *Introduction to the Devout Life.* Theology, like medicine or law, is necessarily a complicated and complicating process, but the real way of the spirit is an uncluttered approach to things. It is the simple way that enables people of good will, in spite of all the confusing changes, stresses, and burdens of the times, to rediscover the true simplicity of the one trustworthy source: the real message of the gospel.

In general, and not just in relation to the particular aspect of Thérèse's thought and practice we are concerned with here, this simplicity is a characteristic of the form of devotion we have been talking about, though above all of devotion to Mary. In this wholly appropriate form of Marian piety, Our Lady is an utterly uncomplicated figure. We might even say that through it she is indeed "demythologized" without having to demythologize her in the ways we have become accustomed to in late nineteenth-century and early twentieth-century critical theology and scholarship. She teaches us to find ourselves by losing ourselves. She does so, not so much through the heroic power and undaunted resolution for which she may stand, but by grace in two senses of the word: by grace as a gift and in the form of what one can only call a kind of "graceful," or gentle and patient, subtlety. She has a unique ability (which she passes on to us) to untie even the most Gordian of knots, and to melt the most resistant and rebellious of hearts. In short, she can smile, and smiling is the perfect symbol of grace which makes all things possible.

Thérèse's life, like that of Mary, developed in quite ordinary circumstances, with apparently extraordinary ease and without any dash or glamour. As far as we can interpret her writings and guess at what her life was actually like, her character was very close to Mary's. Her temperament and personality seem much more in line with what we suspect Mary's to have been than the disposition and character of a saint like Teresa of Avila. To an extent that is very rare among the saints, Thérèse's nature resembled that of the Virgin Mary as reported to us by St Luke. Both of these young women had something very straightforward, clearly defined, and exquisitely fresh about them. Theirs were characters without little side-paths, or knots and complexities. Their wisdom consisted of wholehearted concentration on what really matters, which might easily become moments of exultation or, just as effortlessly, so it seems, pass into silence. Both of them were utterly willing to be guided by the power of signs when they were vouchsafed them, yet never themselves set out to look for, let alone try to determine, the nature and occasions of such moments of grace. These are not, to be sure, the only characteristics of these two very congruous natures. All I have tried to do here is to sketch the main lines of their similarities.

*   *   *

Of course, if we try to find one unique Marian side to Thérèse's character, we shall search in vain. Thérèse's life certainly offers us no text-book prescriptions for following some kind of Marian way to truth; or, at least, a proficient investigation designed to find and write such guidelines would take a lifetime. What we can discover in Thérèse, and without great difficulty, is a Marian way of life.

We may also justly say that the "non-ecstatic" death of Thérèse, as well as Mary's death as certain mystics have described it, have a great deal in common. Several of these mystics have described the dormition, or passing on, of Our Lady, not as a "flight of the soul" or "ascent of the spirit," but as a gentle passage from one point or state to another. Gibieuf, for instance, says: "And her Son so intensified that holy quietude that the soul departed from what it had enlivened to reside in what it loved. Having withdrawn entirely into Jesus, its one and only love, the body which it had inspired with life until that moment remained without movement and without life."

Essentially, however, we may conclude that Thérèse's existence was Marian not in any doctrinally or intellectually definable way, but in the profundity of her very being. In fact, any proficient consideration of Thérèse must give us an approximate idea of what the Virgin Mary was historically. Thérèse did not wish or try to imitate Our Lady in specific ways or by certain practices. Instead, she may be said merely to have discovered that she was like Mary, as if by virtue of some additional quality or hitherto unexplored borderland of being who she actually was, which is indeed the privilege of love pure and simple.

Thérèse and Everlasting Life

Almost forty years ago now I was extremely interested in the subject of the relations between eternity and time. My reflections on this theme were largely inspired by St Augustine's powerful examination of it, but I had also been reading, with vast admiration and respect, Thérèse's *Story of a Soul*. From time to time in the course of my work, the beginnings of a comparison between St Augustine and St Thérèse of the Child Jesus emerged. When I was thinking about the famous event known as the "ecstasy of Ostia," when Augustine and his mother Monica felt for one wonderful mystical moment that they had grasped the very basis and meaning of life eternal, I was amazed to discover in just a very few lines written by this very young Carmelite something extraordinarily pertinent to the life of one of the greatest and most experienced saints in the history of the Church. Thérèse can scarcely be said to have been marked by any experience of the pleasures of the world, and she had undergone nothing comparable to Augustine's education in classical literature and philosophy, let alone his years of rigorous, indeed exhaustive, study of all possible aspects of the topic. Nevertheless she had a wonderfully intuitive understanding of the connections between everlasting life and the mere transient and even pathetic trace of it which we call time.

I had noticed that, very early on, Thérèse had read a work entitled *The End of the World* by a writer unknown to me (and, it seemed, to anyone else) called Fr Arminjon. The full title is *The End of the Present World and the Mysteries of the Future Life*; it was published in 1881. At the time I made a mental note to track down this odd-sounding book one day and to try to discover who Arminjon exactly was. His rather strange name attracted me in some weird way. Who can say why? I happened to visit the Carmel of Lisieux about fifty-two years ago. They very carefully handed me a precious copy of Arminjon's almost totally unobtainable book, which had never been reprinted or reissued in any way. I read it until late into the night. I copied out several extracts, for the nuns utterly refused to lend me the volume, which they treated as one of the treasures of the Carmel. I think I told Céline how very interesting I had found the book, and that it should certainly be republished some day. She smiled very sweetly, raising her stick at the same time.

That day did come. At this very moment, I am looking at a copy of the reprint of the book with an excellent preface which mentions Fr Combes, the doyen of Thérèse studies. I have tried to recall what I thought when I first read Arminjon's work. At that time I was trying to write something like a commentary, or marginal gloss, on what Thérèse had to say about time. Her remarks occur in a short passage on what Augustine, talking with Monica on the river bank at Ostia, called the "everlasting life of the saints."

Arminjon's book is both annoying and superb. It is a mixture of simplistic remarks, quite ghastly errors, really weird, over-the-top, and almost unhealthy opinions and ideas, yet at the same time unusual, astonishing, and sometimes sublime intuitions. We must remember, of course, that this kind of hotch-potch is characteristic of any non-inspired writing that talks about the future; and even more so when it is concerned with the end of all futures. You have only to think of science-fiction novels to understand what I mean. But somehow this very mixture can have a supremely evocative and stimulating effect on the imagination. Something in a fresh, relatively uneducated mind seizes on the brilliant insights amidst all the tawdry clap-trap, fishes them out, works away on them, and produces something new and worthwhile. It is not difficult to understand how these two young girls were so moved by and enthusiastic about Arminjon's work.

What is most interesting in all this bears out what I have already said about Thérèse's particular intellect and sensibility. Both she and Arminjon had an ability to seize on what is really essential. Reading this mixture of dross and superb good sense, she filleted it until she had isolated everything really important, then produced the pure essence of Arminjon and became more Arminjonian than Arminjon himself.

I shall not mention all the things in the book that I find weak, exaggerated, rhetorical, and just inept. But it also contains prophecies, such as a section on the "Chinese peril" which it is very strange to reread at this point in time, considering that the author published his work in 1881:

China is an immense empire with a teeming population. Each day the seas and rivers alone consume a vast overflow of human beings. It is a country which never adequately manages to use its rich and potentially fruitful soil to the best advantage, yet China has its engineers and technicians, and is aware of our stategy and industrial progress. The wars in which we have been engaged recently surely only go to show that in the future the final victory will eventually be granted to those with the masses on their side. In armed conflict as in the political sphere, it is the mechanical and brutal law of weight of numbers that will decide who is successful and who actually wins at the end of the day.

It is easily possible to foresee the far-off day when these millions of pagans who inhabit eastern and northern Asia will possess more soldiers, more arms, and more implements of war than all other nations put together. We can predict a time when they will exploit their numbers and their power to the full, and unleash their immense hordes on our decadent Europe abandoned by God. The invasions we shall suffer then will be inconceivably more terrible and devastating than those of the Vandals and the Huns. They will sack our provinces, violate our rights, destroy every little nation and turn all

in their path to dust and ashes. Then we shall see the rise
of a vast agglomeration consisting of all the inhabitants of
the earth under the rule of a single leader.

This is not the only page of such prophecies to be found in the
work of this latter-day Isaiah. Somehow Arminjon understood the import of the already amazing developments of
technology, and knew how to bring the world of science to
bear on his theological deductions. He looked ahead to the
extraordinary changes that would take place, such as the
human conquest of space, and to a time that would yield
inventions much more effective even than electricity. Admittedly there was a Jules Verne side to him. But he went far
beyond Verne in imagining the human race under a single
regime which would be much more evil than beneficial. We
must remember that Arminjon was prophesying these things
over a hundred years ago, when the poet and novelist Victor
Hugo, the theologian and critical biographer of Christ, Ernest
Renan, the biologist and philosopher Haeckel, the economist
and political philosopher Karl Marx, and so many others,
were almost all promising humanity a future of infinite happiness when science would have put an end to barbarism. At a
time when the greatest minds of the day were preaching the
gospel of infinite progress, Canon Arminjon of Chambéry
was optimistically foretelling the end (certainly quite imminent) of things as they were. There was no perceptible res-
ponse to his warnings, even in the far-off mountainous region
where he taught in a major seminary. He put a letter in a
bottle and dropped it into the ocean of time.

A young girl, on the Norman coast of that immensity,
plucked it out of the waves: "What is this elixir, O fisherman,
beneath the skies? It is knowledge and truth, fisherman, that
meets your eyes!"

The unforgettable lines of Alfred de Vigny, the French
Romantic poet, which other writers always find so comfort-
ing, always appear before my mind's eye when I imagine

Thérèse reading Arminjon. Then I think of all those preachers without congregations, novelists (such as Stendhal) without the public they deserved, poets (such as Rimbaud) without an admiring literary coterie, and mystics without imitators and followers (such as Grignion de Montfort), who have shown that time, chance, and fate—in other words divine patience— do indeed smile on their intuitions and will see them fulfilled.

But is it ever possible to say what a child, however perceptive, has gleaned from the work of a prophet? In this case, I think it is.

What did Thérèse take from her quaint master? Primarily, a certain lyrical style which she perhaps adopted unconsciously and intuitively but made her own. Arminjon's language sometimes reaches the point of what one can only call paroxysm. He stretches his bow until, occasionally, the string breaks. His nervous, elevated style sometimes approaches the level of that of his contemporary, the German philosopher Nietzsche, or that of the inspired French Catholic novelist Léon Bloy. Even though he had nothing approaching the profundity and talent of these great figures, our Arminjon certainly had fire in his belly.

Arminjon's style is perfectly suited to his vital message and intentions. He knew well, and said, that to pierce the indifference and lethargy of the people of his own time who were interested only in the ground under their feet, and often in no more than base material things, it was necessary to cure discord by discord. Otherwise the essential truths could not shine out unmistakably. "Jesus Christ is understood most effectively when he speaks most eloquently, when his teaching is heard whole and entire and the insurpassable glories of his being God himself force themselves upon us." ". . . force themselves upon us," indeed! Like the divinely inspired Catholic poet Paul Claudel, Arminjon might well take as his watchword the line from Thomas Aquinas' great eucharistic hymn, *Lauda Sion*:

QUANTUM POTES, TANTUM AUDE.
Dare the impossible for God's sake.

No one could deny Thérèse's essential charm, but we must never forget that it is charm of a diamond-hard intensity. Though her language was childlike, in the best sense of the word, the thought which it bore flew like an arrow from her to reach its target with what one can only call a burning and passionate exactitude. This is comparable only, in my reading, to an analogous quality in St Catherine of Genoa. I am certain that this was an important aspect of Thérèse's natural abilities, but I am just as certain that the assurance she needed to express this vital intensity and concern came from her reading of Arminjon. She must have thought that Arminjon was a great writer, and in the way of things when one is impressed by great writing, Arminjon somehow gave her the authority to be herself or, to put it in more contemporary language, to do her own thing.

For example, we need only look at the passage from Arminjon which Thérèse copied out on 30 May 1887 and which she kept in her breviary:

> A human being enthused by the fire of divine love is so indifferent to both glory and ignominy that he or she might stand alone with no witness whatsoever to what he or she does. Such a person ignores all temptations. Such a person no longer cares about any suffering whatsoever, treating it as if someone utterly remote had to bear it instead. Whatever the world finds beguiling and infinitely delightful, has no appeal for such a person. He or she is no longer susceptible to the attractions of any material thing, to such an extent that the most precious metal or jewel cannot detract or shatter his or her determination. Such are the effects of divine love when it takes complete hold of a human soul who responds to it with all his or her power and strength. (*Oeuvres complètes* [Complete Works], p. 1210).

The other way in which Canon Arminjon helped the young Thérèse to emerge from the bounds of her tiny provincial and unassumingly middle-class world was to enlarge her visionary capacity to an almost infinite extent. Arminjon had a feeling for infinite spaces. He matched this (as I shall show) with a sense of infinite time. He also had something very unusual and of a quite different order—an understanding of all that was infinite within infinity itself. He possessed something like that feeling for tragedy which only the best dramatists have, and which refines, enlivens, and deepens a feeling for the nature of history that is essential to an artist of real calibre. Such unusual gifts that extend the capacity of intuition and understanding are not met with very often. At the very same time, Victor Hugo in the last section of his *Legend of the Centuries* was exercising the very same ability to look back and forth in time and to put what he described in a setting of infinity. Of course Arminjon was no Victor Hugo as far as literary talent went, but I dare to say that he had a sense of truth that we cannot find in the poet. To Céline and Thérèse who, within the confines of their tiny little world, had no access at all to culture of a higher order, Arminjon offered a visionary depth and fullness that otherwise would have developed only after years of study and immersion in a very different kind of literature and philosophy. Their minds and souls enjoyed the fruits of culture and knowledge without all that effort, merely by reading the humble Canon's works.

I come now to the third lesson which Thérèse gleaned from Arminjon. It is more important than the first two and takes me straight to the heart of my subject: a sense of the way in which time is connected with eternity. Reading with such intensity, Thérèse arrived at what one can only call a Pascalian intuition of the relationship between the finite and the infinite. She came to understand, in other words, that the finite disappears in the presence of the infinite. Time, however long, however various, however rich it may be, is absolutely nothing in the face of eternity. Confronted with eternity, this present time shows its true nature. It discloses its immersion, absorption, and interest in itself alone. It reveals its total inability to satisfy, explain, and hold the meaning and passionate ascent of the free spirit, or to catch, pin down, and characterize the future. The phrase "for ever and ever" (*per omnia saecula saeculorum*) is one of the most famous but of course ultimately inadequate attempts to express this infinitude of infinity. In geometry it is not an indefinitely extended line which comes closest to a perfect expression of eternity but a point, or stop.

We all know in some way what infinity really means, however incapable most of us are of any exercise of the mind or spirit that dispenses with symbols, representations, and images. I am sure that a seven-year-old child would know exactly what I have in mind. Any proficient teacher would have no difficulty in explaining this problem of problems to the limpid mind of someone of that age.

But it is an entirely different proposition to explain the point in question in the terms proper to geometry, philosophy, or even the ordinary everyday language of a well-educated person. It is also a quite different project to try to translate intuition into passionately clear and powerfully, immediately accessible language, after it has undergone that strange interior journey from one's mind and soul to one's heart. Apart from the works of St Augustine, I do not know of any text which is more illuminating, authentic, powerfully charged, and affective in that respect than these lines which so enraptured our Child-philosopher:

> The Lord loves his own chosen souls more ardently than any mother has loved her dearest child, but that means that he must express his own integrity and devotion to them by never allowing their devotion and self-giving to outweigh and, as it were, defeat his own infinite love.
>
> Indeed, the Lord can never forget that the saints,

when they walked on earth, offered him the homage and unstinting surrender of their entire selves, of all their quietude and all their joys. He never ignores the fact that they longed with all their hearts for their veins to fill with an inexhaustible flow of blood, so that they could spend it, if necessary, as a vital and invincible token of their faith. He knows that in the very depths of themselves they longed to have a thousand hearts rather than just one, so that they could feel as passionately as they did a thousand times over, and that they longed to possess a thousand bodies to be martyred over and over again and to rise unvanquished as many times from their trials. Yet, though he knows and acknowledges all this, God declares:

"Now it is my turn . . . the only way that I can respond to these saints who have offered me themselves and their very selves is to give my own Self, without limit or restraint. If I placed the very sceptre of creation in their hands, and if I infused them with my illuminating power, I would do more for them than they would ever long or hope for. But even if I were to do that, I should never exhaust the possibilities of all that I wish to do for them in the infinite reaches and possibilities of my Heart. I am willing to give them more than paradise, more than all the riches of my knowledge. I offer them my life, nature, and eternal and infinite substance of being. If I welcome my followers and friends into my own house, if I comfort them and watch their joy as I embrace them with my loving-kindness, I do so to satisfy their thirst and their longings more generously than ever they could have thought possible, more abundantly than ever they could need if their hearts are to find perfect peace and fulfillment. Yet all this is inadequate and can never satisfy my divine Heart, can never perfectly fulfill and satisfy my love. I must be the soul of their soul. I have to enter into them and fill them with my Godhead just as fiery heat infuses iron with its glow and ardour, until I show myself to their minds and spirits without any cloud, veil or any mediation of the bodily senses. I must do so until I am united with them in an everlasting encounter and they know me face to face, so that my glory enlightens them, and is expressed and shines forth from every pore of their being. Then they will 'know me as I know them and become like unto Gods themselves.'"(*ibid.*, p. 201)

This text ends with the idea that creation tends towards the point where human beings become gods. It is very like a concept in *The Two Sources of Morality and Religion* (1932), by the French philosopher Henri Bergson. In the course of examining the relation between morals and religion, Bergson concludes that creative energy is best defined as love, and that creation is the process by which God brings into being "creators, in order to have, beside himself, beings worthy of his love." In other words, the goal of creation is the authentic coming into being of human beings and their transformation through love. At the end of the book Bergson speaks of technology as the gradual building up of one body of humankind on the levels of material civilization and of science, and of mystical religion infusing a soul into this body. An influx of divine love brings about, as it were, a deified humanity, for it transforms the universe into "a machine for the making of gods." Bergson, wiser than Arminjon, did not put a capital letter on "gods." This text of Arminjon's is very similar to another passage in his work which Thérèse did not copy but certainly read; it had an immense effect on her:

"The superabundant joy which my divine vision will give to the elect will be beyond the level of the most unutterable joys. It will be a veritable torrent of pleasure and intensity, life in all its inexhaustible richness and the very source of all well-being and of all vitality." "How precious is your steadfast love, O God! All people may take refuge in the shadow of your wings. They feast on the abundance of your house, and you give them drink from the river of your delights. For with you is the fountain of life; in your light we see light": *Quemadmodum multipli-*

casti misericordiam tuam, Deus. Filii atem hominum in tegmine alarum tuarum sperabunt. Inebriabuntur ab ubertate domus tuae, et torrente voluptatis tuae potabis eos; quoniam apud te est fons vitae, et in lumine tuo videbimus lumen (Ps. 36:7-9). It will be as if, as St Augustine says, God were to transfer his own Heart to us, so that we could love and rejoice with all the energy of the love and joys of God himself: *Erit voluntati plenitudo pacis*—"For then all human longing will be assuaged. . . ."

Eternal life, says St Paul, is like a vast collection and onrush of all delights, intoxications and pleasures: *Aeternum Gloriae pondus*: all the weight of love will re-enliven human beings to the point at which they are cancelled as that which they merely were, and it will inexhaustibly renew and supplement their youth and strength. Eternal life is a never-ending spring from which the soul draws vast draughts of essence and life. It is a marriage feast in which the soul embraces its Creator in an eternal embrace, without any relaxation of the intensity of this moment in which for the first time it is united with God and holds him to its very self for ever (pp. 206-15).

Yet the elect when they see God will not understand him, for, as the Lateran Council teaches us, "No created mind can comprehend God." We shall see God as he really is, some of us more, and some of us less, in accordance with our dispositions and our merits. For we cannot even say theologically that the Immaculate Virgin herself, who sees God more clearly and more perfectly than all the angels and all the saints together, could ever succeed in seeing him and knowing him fully. God is infinite and all we can say is that a human being will see him, and will see him appropriately, as he is, *sicuti est in integro*. Yet at the same time human beings will not see him in the sense of managing to discover all aspects of his perfection; to know him as the eternal Being contemplating Himself in all the splendour of his Word and in the unity of his love with the Holy Spirit. If I may be allowed to use a crude and inadequate image to illustrate this point (not forgetting that all analogies borrowed from the world of living things are without any power of proportion or similitude when transferred to the realm of uncreated being), we may say that in relation to God the elect are like a traveller standing on the shore of the Atlantic Ocean. The traveller knows that it is the ocean and with his or her human eyes can see the ocean extending and moving towards infinity. He or she may say: "I have seen the ocean" and yet there will be reefs and far-distant islands that our traveller has never seen and will never know, for he or she cannot know even the majority of, let alone all, the shores, bays and inlets of this mighty sea.

The contemplation of God will not be an immobile state. Above all, it will be activity, an infinite ascent in which movement and rest will be mysteriously joined together.

Perhaps it will help us to understand this more proficiently if we think of a sage endowed from birth with wings. He or she is able to visit and survey every corner of the stars and penetrate the atmosphere of every planet in the universe. He or she is able to explore all the wonders hidden in the numberless constellations that lie even beyond those that twinkle in the night sky. Our wise person travels from universe to universe, and from planet to planet within them. As he or she penetrates all the more aspects of the immensity of worlds and worlds beyond worlds, surprise after surprise, thrill after thrill, is encountered. He or she incessantly comes upon sights more amazing and marvellous than any already seen and, in doing so, sees unfold before him or her the beginnings of even more vast and more beguiling prospects. One day, however, even for our experienced space-traveller, a moment will come when he or she comes to rest on the shores of the very last world of all worlds. The infinite, however, has no ultimate shore, no last grain of sand upon its final beach for our tourist through space to touch down upon. The fortunate mariners who undertake this last voyage we all must take into infinity will sail in an immeasurable endlessness of light and love, so endlessly endless that they will never cry out like Christopher Columbus: "Land! Land!" Instead they will say: "God, God for ever, God again and again...!" "And new perfection will follow new perfection for ever and for ever" (p. 207).

"O happy state of paradise!" St Augustine says in this respect, where there will be as many heavens as there are citizens of paradise, and where glory will be ours by as many channels as there are hearts to take note of us and care for us, and where we shall own as many kingdoms as there will be monarchs concerned to reward us. The joy to come will be commensurate with the number of those who receive it (*Quot socii, tot gaudia*) (p. 216).

All the foregoing is perfectly clear in one sense but needs to be elucidated in some respects.

1. Arminjon multiplies the infinite by the infinite. This does not accord entirely with Pascal, for whom the happiness of heaven is an infinity of joy in the present moment multiplied by an infinity of moments ("joy eternal in return for a single day of earthly behaviour"). Arminjon develops the ideas of SS Paul and John. The happiness of the elect is not a form of happiness that the human heart could conceive and desire but a form of happiness that our hearts, however expansive they may be, could never conceive of or even desire. There is, says God, "nothing other than paradise in heaven," nothing more than the gift of what is quite other than me (my life, my nature, my everlasting substance): "It is necessary," God says, "for me to feed them with my Godhead, for me to unite with them in an everlasting encounter in which we know one another face to face." This is a very expressive comment on the teaching of St Paul: ". . . as it is written, 'What no eye has seen, nor ear heard, nor the human heart conceived, what God has prepared for those who love him'— these things God has revealed to us through the Spirit; for the Spirit searches everything, even the depths of God . . . we

speak of these things in words not taught by human wisdom but taught by the Spirit interpreting spiritual things to those who are spiritual" (1 Cor. 2:9-13); of St Peter: "By his great mercy he has given us a new birth into a living hope through the resurrection of Jesus Christ from the dead, and into an inheritance that is imperishable, undefiled, and unfading, kept in heaven for you, who are being protected by the power of God through faith for a salvation ready to be revealed in the last time . . . things into which angels long to look!" (1 Pet. 1:4-12); and of St John: "Beloved, we are God's children now; what we will be has not yet been revealed. What we do know is this: when he is revealed, we will be like him, for we will see him as he is" (1 John 3:2). What Arminjon does is to fit the teaching of these passages and their contexts to the mental capacity of two girls in late nineteenth-century provincial France.

2. The vision by which this experience of eternal life is anticipated is designed to transform our awareness of the way in which history works.

Arminjon is captivated by the idea that history as a whole is no more than a mere moment when conceived duly, that is, in comparison with eternity. Consequently, real history is not this rapid yet ambiguous phantasmagoria in which we are situated and which seems to speed us along with it. Instead, history seen properly is universal history as a whole; history complete and with judgment passed upon it. What Arminjon says in this respect is worthy of the great French thinker Joseph de Maistre, who had a supreme ability to encapsulate complex thoughts in a few words: "History is not at an end; it will start in the valley of Jehoshaphat" (the "valley of decision" [Joel 4:2, 12], where God passes an apocalyptic judgment upon the nations; *Jehoshaphat* = "God is judge").

Arminjon might well have recalled the famous saying of the German philosopher of history, Hegel: "The history of the world is the judgment of the world" (*Weltgeschichte ist Weltgericht*).

Accordingly, part of what "happens" in everlasting life will be souls acting as "witnesses and actors in this supreme drama. All human existence and history will seem so short that we shall think that it lasted hardly even a day" (Arminjon, p. 35). One word in this quotation is rather surprising—"actors."

Of course, we all might easily conclude that the souls in heaven will be witnesses to the history of salvation (which will carry on, so to speak, in the background of their glory and irrespective of their "will" on the subject). But that they should still be "actors," and continue to participate in some way in the fulfillment of creation and the crowning glory of history is a novel suggestion. We know that this was to be one of the favourite ideas of the Child Thérèse. After her merely incidental death, she was sure that she would be able to continue her historical mission.

3. After reading about this luminous prospect in Arminjon's book, Thérèse's conception of the glory of heavenly life became one of a glory shared, communicated, and multiplied by the reciprocal love of all the souls in heaven.

Admittedly, if we looked too curiously into the possible details of this vision of heavenly bliss, we might be led to suspect that the unequal provision of graces, merits, and blessings could cause certain difficulties. There would be the possibility, for instance, of a kind of everlasting shadow on the happiness of all those not vouchsafed the most delirious extremes of sacred joy. Surely this would cause something like a holy envy; a sort of heavenly regret, then, but an everlasting regret in a state in which nothing will ever change again? In other words, the idea of different degrees of glory runs the risk of introducing a form of inequality into the courts of heaven which, unlike earthly inequality, would be absolute and without the consolations of transience and the possibility of redress in the future.

But Thérèse took from Arminjon the saving conviction that

perfect and eternal happiness includes a communion and community of love.

Anyone who has enjoyed even a taste of something approximating to that state of things will know that it comes from the Giver of all good gifts, and that accordingly it is given to us so that we may give it to others. In heaven, therefore, which must be a place without (even spiritual) envy or jealousy, anyone who has more to give will give that more to those who have less, and who will then enjoy the perfect satisfaction of their longing.

I have already mentioned, when speaking of the Virgin Mary, this reversal of roles, which is one of the most welcome and kindest fruits of love. But Arminjon also stresses the notion that in heaven every single person will bring pleasure and joy to another by exercising his or her own particular, historically-given ability or gift, so that the specialisms (so to speak) of our earthly functions (which will have made this one a martyr, that one a holy virgin, and that one a married man or woman) will be brought into due and proper relationship one to another by the overwhelming power of love. Our gifts will no longer be compared with those of others or, as sometimes happens all too often, used to denigrate them.

As the economy and process of divine history demands, "each person will be made rich by the riches that belong to all."

* * *

There are many other interesting points to be gleaned from Arminjon's works that throw light on Thérèse's conception of the religious way and eternal life. I have drawn attention only to the most salient and important of them for defining the main lines of her personality and approach.

In the life of St Augustine there was a uniquely rich moment, the *momentum intelligentiae*, or moment of truth, when, together with his mother Monica, he believed that he had come into contact with eternal life. This fleeting yet abundantly rich moment, stored in his extraordinary memory, became the concealed point of power and light throughout his work. When Céline and Thérèse read Arminjon's book at the Belvédère, or gazebo in a commanding position (their "terrace of Ostia"), an eminence from which, in more senses than one, they had a vast and illuminating prospect, they experienced their own "moment of truth," a kind of quiet ecstasy which provided them with a similar reference-point of light and power thereafter. Thérèse, who took every brilliant insight all the way to its ultimate conclusion, decided after reading this passage that henceforth she would live only in and for eternity, even though she was compelled still to live as an ordinary human being in human time. That was her vocation as a Carmelite, separated or, rather, detached from everything in order all the more effectively to devote herself whole and entire to others.

It is scarcely surprising that, when they had read St Augustine's *Confessions*, Céline and Thérèse compared their own experience to the famous Ostian "ecstasy" of the bishop of Hippo. The comparison seems all the more apt when we remember that Canon Arminjon based his commentaries on the state of the blessed in heaven on Augustine's works. We may even go so far as to say that one of the great effects in modern times of Augustine's ecstatic experience was this moment of transformation that took place in the house at Lisieux. Many erudite works have been and will be written on the implications of Augustine's mystical experience, but few if any of them could match the effect it has had in and through the mediation of Thérèse's life and writings. It is impossible nowadays to visit the Belvédère at Les Buissonnets, which was like a kind of mystical beacon in Thérèse's life, without thinking of the way in which Augustine and his mother looked out to the limitless waters of eternity, towards the mouth of the Tiber, that pallid river which Saint Peter ascended on his way to Rome and the foundation of the great city of faith, as Virgil unknowingly prophesied when writing his epic poem on the journeys of Aeneas.

Very often, an exceptional person finds his or her unique self with the help of a rather ordinary individual. The minor note is necessary for the full effect of the major sound. Every tale about a hero is replete with events like this in which the wonderful being wins through to his or her extraordinary deeds or state of being only with the help of humble little people. Thérèse has had countless spiritual heirs and descendants. But, strange to say, she also had predecessors who henceforth, like her father and mother, are important in a way only because of her, and thus may be said, however paradoxical this may seem, to descend from her. This was exactly what happened when she gave Canon Arminjon of Chambéry a new lease of life by including him in the company of her predecessors reborn as her spiritual children. She did so by revealing the luminous power of the insights concealed in his work, and transforming them into the central ideas of her own writings.

It would not be excessive, however, to say that in certain respects Arminjon is more to the point than Thérèse.

Thérèse certainly lived in a period at the end of a century that was quite as captivated by a dream as the France of Louis XV and Louis XVI. It was an individualistic and optimistic century that believed in infinite progress. A mystical spirit, to be sure, can rise above such illusions. A mystic is able to ward off all real anxiety and anguish by accepting even the most extreme suffering willingly and cheerfully. When we read Thérèse in our nuclear age she seems totally removed from the harsh concerns of these times. Of course, it would not be difficult to play a few tricks with her writings, to bring her message up to date, and to give it an eschatological dimension that seemed to fit the horrors and fears of the moment. But there is no foundation for that in her actual words.

On the other hand, if you remove all the rhetoric and read

the real Arminjon, you find an amazingly modern author underneath the time-bound phraseology. He never talks, to be sure, about the atom bomb, but he does speak of the possible destruction of the universe by fire. He opens up the prospect of an end to the material world, even though he assures us that it is not radically imminent. He foresees, so it seems, the discoveries of our first space travellers, even looking ahead to a point when a vast multitude of stars of every shape and size will have been visited and reconnoitred by human beings. He looks forward to new types of world government. He anticipates the arrival of new political powers based on forms of technological atheism. He sees very well that science itself will eventually detect not a material universe whose promise will last forever but a gradually degrading universe, and therefore the mathematical probability of its end. I have already mentioned what Arminjon said about the possible relations with the West of a newly powerful, atheistic, and ever more densely-populated China. However, even if we ignore these details we cannot fail to be impressed when reading Arminjon nowadays by his sense of eschatology and community. These particular emphases are very much in line with certain aspects of current thought and, though we do not find them repeated word for word in what Thérèse actually wrote, she undoubtedly read them and they remain in the background, so to speak, of what she says. They interestingly complement the essential ideas that she drew from her mentor's work, and reworked and emphasized so memorably for her own and our edification.

The insights of the percipient author of *The End of the World as it is and The Mysteries of the Life to Come* shine out still in the life and works of Thérèse of the Child Jesus to enlighten us and many who will come after us. There are truly many mansions in the kingdom of heaven.

Chronology of Thérèse's Life

1873

2 January
11.30 p.m: Thérèse is born to Louis Martin, a watchmaker, and Zélie-Marie Martin, a lace-maker, at 36 (now 42) Rue Saint-Blaise, Alençon, Normandy. She is the youngest of five children. Her sisters are Marie, Pauline, Léonie, and Céline.

4 January
She is baptized Marie-Françoise-Thérèse Martin at the church of Notre Dame. Her godmother is her eldest sister Marie, and her godfather Paul Albert Boul, son of a friend of Louis Martin.

14 January
She smiles at her mother for the first time.

17 January
Thérèse shows the first symptoms of enteritis.

1 March
Thérèse suffers a more intense attack of enteritis.

16 March
Thérèse's mother can no longer breast-feed her. Because of ill health, Thérèse goes to stay with a wet nurse, Rose Taillé, and her family at Sémallé, a small hamlet amidst woods and pastureland several miles outside Alençon. She sees her parents every Thursday when her nurse comes to the market to sell butter and eggs.

1874

2 April
Thérèse returns to live with her family in Alençon.

1875

14 March
Thérèse's mother writes to her sister-in-law Céline, telling her that at two years and three months Thérèse ran from the house toward the church. At home, she cried for an hour because she had not been to Mass.

March
Thérèse takes her first train to visit her aunt, Sr

Marie-Dosithée, at the Convent of the Visitation in Mans. Thérèse has a fit of tears on entering the convent. She recovers her composure and captivates the nuns.

1876

December   Zélie Martin consults a doctor. She learns that she has advanced breast cancer, and that nothing short of a miracle can save her.

May   Zélie visits Lourdes with Marie, Pauline, and Léonie.

August   During the last days of their mother's agonizing illness Thérèse and Céline are sent every day to Mme Leriche, a niece of Louis Martin.

27-28 August   At 12.30 a.m. Thérèse's mother dies of cancer. In the morning Louis Martin takes Thérèse to give her mother a final kiss. "I said nothing but pressed my lips on the forehead of my darling mother. I do not remember crying very much, I did not tell anyone how deeply I felt. . . . I looked and listened in silence. . . ."

16 November   The Martin family move to Les Buissonnets in Lisieux (in the Calvados district of Normandy).

1878

August   Thérèse and her family spend the summer holiday at Trouville with their mother's family, the Guérins. Thérèse writes: "I will never forget the impression that the sea made on me. I was fascinated by its vastness, the roaring of the waves, and my soul was full of a sense of God's grandeur and power."

1879

December, or January 1880

When six years old, Thérèse makes her first Confession at St Peter's Cathedral. She leaves the confessional feeling "happy and light-hearted."

1881

3 October   Thérèse joins her sister Céline at the Benedictine Abbey in Lisieux. Previously she had been taught at home by her two elder sisters, Marie and Pauline.

1882

2 October   Thérèse's elder sister Pauline enters the Carmelite Convent of Lisieux and becomes Sr Agnes of Jesus. Louis Martin pays a `dowry of eight thousand francs.

1883

March   Louis Martin leaves with Marie and Léonie for a visit to Paris. Thérèse and Céline are sent to the Guérin family during their absence. Thérèse becomes ill and shows signs of "strange trembling."

6 April   Thérèse recovers slightly and attends her sister Pauline's clothing ceremony.

7 April   Thérèse is sick again. M. Martin makes a series of novenas, the last at the church of Our Lady of Victories in Paris.

13 May   On Pentecost Sunday the delirious Thérèse notices a smile on the face of the statue of Our Lady of Victories in her room, and attributes her recovery from illness to Our Lady's intervention. She possibly thinks that she has been granted an appearance of the Virgin and that the intervention is miraculous.

20 August - 30 September

Louis Martin takes his daughters to Alençon for a holiday. Their first visit is to the cemetery where their mother is buried.

22 August   Thérèse is introduced to Marie's spiritual director, Fr Pichon, S.J. He finds her artless and innocent, self-effacing and considerate to others: "She was shy and reserved, and never put herself first."

1884

4 - 8 May	Thérèse makes a retreat at her school, led by Fr Domin. It is her first time away from her sisters. She is unable to get ready in the morning on her own and has to ask the mistress in charge of the dressing-room to comb her hair.
8 May	Thérèse makes her first Communion. She receives the host as a "kiss of love." In the evening Louis Martin takes Thérèse to the Carmelite convent to attend Pauline's profession of faith.
14 June	Thérèse is confirmed by Mgr Hugonin, bishop of Bayeux. Léonie is her godmother.

1885

3 - 10 May	Thérèse spends a holiday at the Chalet des Roses, Deauville.
15 - 21 May	Thérèse prepares for her solemn commemoration of her first Communion. She makes a retreat at her school under Fr Domin's direction. During the retreat she has an attack of scruples.

1886

February	Thérèse is unhappy at school without Céline and gets her father's permission to leave the Benedictines. She becomes a private student at Mme Papinau's in Lisieux.
July	Thérèse leaves for the holidays at Trouville with the Guérins. After three days she is upset by their criticisms and returns to Lisieux.
July	Thérèse learns that Marie is to join the Carmelites. She is very unhappy at the prospect of losing her sister: "As soon as I learnt of Marie's decision, I made up my mind not to look for enjoyment in this world any longer."
15 October	At twenty-six years of age, Thérèse's eldest sister, Marie (their surrogate mother since the

death of Mme Martin), enters the Carmelite convent of Lisieux and takes the name in religion, Sr Marie of the Sacred Heart. Louis Martin pays a dowry of eight thousand francs.

1 December   Léonie returns home after an abortive attempt to become a Poor Clare at Alençon.

25 December   Thérèse prays for a miracle to help her overcome her constant tearful episodes. Her prayers are granted.

1887

1 May   Louis Martin has a transient attack of paralysis.

May   Thérèse reads and is greatly influenced by *La Fin du monde présent et les mystères de la vie future* ("The End of the Present World and the Mysteries of the Future Life") by Canon Arminjon.

29 May   Thérèse tells her father that she wants to become a Carmelite nun.

13 July   Thérèse learns about the unrepentant murderer, Henri Pranzini, who has been condemned to death. She prays for his repentance.

16 July   Léonie enters the Carmelite convent in Caen for the first time.

31 August   Moments before his execution, Pranzini kisses the crucifix offered to him by the priest accompanying him to the guillotine. Thérèse reads about this in *La Croix* and takes this as a sign that God has answered her prayers. She calls Pranzini her "first child."

31 October   Thérèse, accompanied by her father, appeals to the bishop of Bayeux, Mgr Hugonin, to be allowed to enter the Carmelite convent.

4 November   Thérèse, her father, and Céline stop off in Paris on their way to Rome. They visit the usual sights but above all various churches. Thérèse is partic-

ularly drawn to Notre-Dame des Victoires (Our Lady of Victories), in the second arrondissement, where she prays to our Lady and to St Joseph to keep her in a state appropriate to her vocation. Thérèse is apprehensive about all the dangers of travel through a world that might compromise the purity of her intention. It is here that she feels completely liberated from her scruples.

7 November	Thérèse, Céline, and her father take the train to Rome from the Gare de l'Est, Paris.
20 November	In Rome, Thérèse's group of pilgrims is granted an audience with Pope Leo XIII. Kneeling before him, she asks his special permission—in honour of his jubilee—to become a Carmelite nun, even though she is only fifteen. He tells her to follow the advice of her superiors. Now extraordinarily courageous, Thérèse insists that one word from the Pope could solve the whole problem. Taken aback, the Pontiff can only offer the vatic comment that she will enter Carmel if God wants her to. Thérèse shows signs of taking her interrogation of the Pope further. Two papal guards and the priest with the group have to remove Thérèse before the Pope becomes unduly irritated.
2 December	Thérèse, her father, and Céline return to Lisieux.
28 December	Mother Marie de Gonzague receives a letter from Mgr Hugonin to say she can admit Thérèse Martin to the convent.

1888

1 January	Thérèse is told that she can enter at Easter.
9 April	On the feast of the Annunciation, aged fifteen years and four months, Thérèse enters the Carmelite convent of Lisieux. Louis Martin pays a dowry of ten thousand francs.
10 April	As a postulant, Thérèse follows the daily time-

table of the Carmelites. She gets up at 4.45 a.m.; 5 - 7a.m.: prayers; 7 a.m.: Mass; 8 a.m.: breakfast of soup, then work; 9.50 a.m: first examination of conscience; 10 a.m.: meal; 11 a.m.: recreation; 12 noon: silence or free time; 1 p.m.: work; 2 p.m.: Vespers; 2.30 p.m.: spiritual reading; 3 p.m.: work; 5 p.m.: prayers; 6 p.m.: supper; 6.45 p.m.: recreation; 7.40 p.m.: last office with recitation of the canticle of Simeon and antiphon of Our Lady; 8 p.m.: silence or free time; 9 p.m.: second examination of conscience; 10.30 or 11 p.m.: bedtime.

16 June	Céline tells her father that she wants to become a nun.
23 June	Louis Martin, who has lost his memory several times, disappears.
27 June	M. Guérin and Céline find M. Martin at Le Havre. He is in a confused state.
November	Louis Martin's mental health declines. He starts to give away large amounts of money. This worries the Guérin family considerably.

1889

5 - 10 January	Thérèse makes a retreat.
10 January	Thérèse is formally clothed as a nun during a ceremony presided over by Bishop Hugonin. She is now Sr Thérèse of the Child Jesus and the Holy Face.
12 February	After brandishing a revolver while undergoing a series of hallucinations, Louis Martin is taken to the Bon-Sauveur, a private mental hospital in Caen, where he stays for three years. Léonie and Céline stay at a boarding-house nearby for several months.

1890

8 September	Thérèse makes her Profession on the feast of Our Lady's Nativity.
24 September	Thérèse takes the veil.

1891

February	Thérèse becomes assistant sacristan under the aegis of Sr Saint Stanislas.
April - July	Thérèse prays for Fr Hyacinthe Loyson.
8 - 15 October	Fr Alexis Prou, a Recollet friar, preaches a retreat at the convent.
5 December	Thérèse is present at the death of Mother Geneviève, the foundress of the convent. She is profoundly moved by her first experience of someone's last moments.

End of December

An outbreak of influenza sweeps through the convent and claims the lives of several elderly nuns.

1892

10 May	Louis Martin, both legs paralyzed, returns to Lisieux.
12 May	Louis Martin visits the convent for the last time.

1893

2 February	At the request of Sr Thérèse of Saint Augustine, Thérèse writes her first poem, entitled *La Rosée divine* ("The Sacred Dew").
20 February	Thérèse's elder sister Pauline (Sr Agnes of Jesus) is elected prioress of the Lisieux convent.
Spring	Thérèse ceases to be assistant sacristan and is appointed assistant mistress of novices. She paints religious watercolours for sale to the public.
24 June	Léonie enters the convent of the Visitation at Caen for a second time.

September	Thérèse is appointed second portress under Sr Raphael.

1894

21 January	Thérèse writes her first play (in which she plays Joan), *The Mission of Joan of Arc*, for the name day of her sister, Pauline, the prioress.
29 July	Louis Martin, Thérèse's father, dies at the castle of La Musse, Eure.
14 September	Céline enters the Carmelite convent and becomes Sr Geneviève of the Holy Face and of Saint Thérèse.
December	The first ideas of Thérèse's "Little Way" emerge from her reading of the Bible.

1895

January	Thérèse starts writing what amounts to her autobiography, *The Story of a Soul*—manuscript A—at the request of her sister Pauline (Mother Agnes of Jesus).
26 February	Thérèse writes a poem entitled *Vivre d'amour* ("To Live a Life of Love"), which she feels best expresses her purpose in life. During this year she writes numerous poems on this theme.
20 July	Léonie leaves the convent of the Visitation.
15 August	Marie Guérin enters the convent at Lisieux.
17 October	Mother Agnes of Jesus makes the seminarist Maurice Bellière Thérèse's "first spiritual brother." Thérèse's task is to help this future missionary by her prayers and sacrifices.

1896

20 January	Thérèse finishes her *Story of a Soul* and presents it to the prioress, Mother Agnes of Jesus, who puts it in a drawer without reading it.
21 January	At the request of Mother Agnes of Jesus, Thérèse

writes a piece on the theme of the flight into Egypt to celebrate the prioress's name day. The prioress does not like the piece and interrupts it before the end. Thérèse is hurt by these two humiliations but, according to Céline, does not react outwardly in any way.

21 March	Mother Marie de Gonzague is re-elected prioress.
2 - 3 April	During the night of Maundy Thursday-Good Friday, Thérèse coughs up blood for the first time.
After Easter	Thérèse experiences her own version of the "dark night of the soul."
10 May	Thérèse has a dream about three Carmelite nuns. One of them is St Teresa of Avila's adviser, Mother Anne of Jesus, who introduced the Teresian reform in France. In the dream, Thérèse asks Mother Anne how much longer she is to spend on earth. She also asks for reassurance that God approves of her "little actions." Mother Anne assures her that she will soon be in heaven and that God asks nothing else of her.
30 May	Mother Marie de Gonzague (the prioress), entrusts Thérèse with a "second spiritual brother," Fr Adolphe Roulland of the Foreign Missions, who is soon leaving for China.
November	Fr Roulland encourages Thérèse to read the biography and correspondence of Fr J. Théophane Vénard, who was beheaded in the citadel of Hanoi in 1861.
December	Mother Marie de Gonzague orders Thérèse to use a fire in her room to ward off the intense cold. She also advises Sr Geneviève to follow the doctor's orders and rub Thérèse's body with a horsehair glove—an ineffective remedy of the time against tuberculosis. Thérèse is told to

have an extra hour in bed: she must get up at 6.40 a.m. instead of 5.45 a.m. In spite of these concessions, Thérèse's health steadily declines. This is reflected in her poem *Comment je veux aimer* ("How I want to love"), written at Sr St John of the Cross' request, and in her Christmas poem *La Volière de l'Enfant Jésus* ("The Birdcage of the Child Jesus").

1897

8 February	Mother Marie de Gonzague asks Thérèse to write a play for the golden jubilee of Sr St Stanislas of the Sacred Heart. In St Stanislaus Kostka's short life (1550-68), Thérèse sees a brother in suffering. They both want to do good on earth after death.
3 March	In spite of her failing health Thérèse tries to fast to mark the beginning of Lent.
March	She writes to Fr Bellière, who reads her poem *Vivre d'amour* and asks to see others. Thérèse replies that "these poor poems will not tell you who I am, but what I would like to be and ought to be." She says that her imminent death will not interrupt her mission to "Love Jesus and make him loved."
19 March	Thérèse writes to Fr Roulland, who fell seriously ill when he got to China. He attributes his recovery to the constant prayers of his spiritual sister.
Early April	Thérèse becomes seriously ill.
6 April	Mother Agnes starts taking down the last words of Thérèse.
8 July	Thérèse is taken to the convent infirmary.
30 July	Thérèse receives the last Sacraments.
15 - 27 August	Thérèse experiences great suffering.
19 August	Thérèse receives Communion for the last time.

30 September	At 7.20 p.m. Thérèse dies, surrounded by the community. Her last words are: "My God, I love you."
4 October	Thérèse is buried in the cemetery of Lisieux.

1898

30 September	Two thousand copies of Thérèse's *The Story of a Soul* are published on the first anniversary of her death.

1899   The first cures and favours are granted to pilgrims visiting her graveside.

1902

19 April	Mother Agnes is re-elected prioress, and with the exception of a period of eighteen months (1908 - 1909), remains so until her death.

1903   Fr Taylor, a Scottish priest, reads Thérèse's *The Story of a Soul,* and visits the Carmelite convent at Lisieux to propose Thérèse's canonization. The nuns are astonished at the idea.

1907   Fr Prévost submits a copy of Thérèse's *The Story of a Soul.* Pope Pius X anticipates Thérèse's canonization and names her the "greatest saint of our time."

1908

26 May	Reine Fauquet, a blind child aged four, is healed at Thérèse's grave.

1914   The Cause of Thérèse's beatification is introduced in Rome.

1921   Pope Benedict XV signs the Decree confirming the heroic virtues of Thérèse; she is now "venerable."

1923

29 April	Thérèse is beatified by Pope Pius XI.

1925

17 May   Thérèse of the Child Jesus is canonized by Pope Pius XI. Her feast day is 3 October.

1927

January   First publication of the *Novissima Verba*. Mother Agnes records her last conversations with Thérèse, between May and September 1897.

14 December   Pope Pius XI names Thérèse Patroness of all Missionaries, together with St Francis Xavier.

1937

11 July   Inauguration and blessing of the basilica of Lisieux by Pope XI's legate, Cardinal Pacelli, the future Pope Pius XII.

1940   Marie Martin dies.

1941   Léonie Martin dies at the convent of the Visitation at Caen.

1944

3 May   Pope Pius XII names Thérèse second Patron of France together with Joan of Arc. Pauline and Céline are present at the ceremony.

1951   Pauline Martin dies.

1956   Publication of the facsimile edition of the autobiographical Manuscripts.

1959   Céline Martin dies.

1980

2 June   Pope John Paul II makes a pilgrimage to Lisieux.

Select Bibliography

A. BY ST THERESE, in English translation

St Thérèse of Lisieux, Her Last Conversations. Trans. J. Clarke, O.C.D.. Washington, 1975.

Saint Thérèse of Lisieux, General Correspondence. Trans. J. Clarke, O.C.D., 2 vols..Washington, 1972, 1988.

Soeur Thérèse of Lisieux, An Autobiography. Ed. T. N. Taylor. London, 1912, revised ed. as *Saint Thérèse of Lisieux, The Little Flower of Jesus.* New York, 1927.

Thérèse of Lisieux: Autobiography of a Saint. Trans. R. A. Knox. London, 1958.

Story of a Soul, The Autobiography of St Thérèse of Lisieux. Trans. J. Clarke, O.C.D.. Washington, 1972. The first translation from the original manuscript.

Collected Letters of Saint Thérèse of of Lisieux. Trans. F. J. Sheed. New York, 1949.

Thérèse of Lisieux—A Discovery of Love. A selection of her writings, ed. T. Carey. London, 1992.

Poems of St Thérèse of Lisieux. Trans. A. Bancroft. London, 1995.

B. ON ST THERESE, in English

H. Petitot. *St Teresa of Lisieux.* London, 1927.

V. Sackville-West. *The Eagle and the Dove.* London, 1943.

H. U. von Balthasar. *St Teresa of Lisieux.* London, 1953.

H. Combes. *The Mission of St Teresa of Lisieux.* London, 1956.

Sr Geneviève of the Holy Face (Céline Martin). *A Memoir of My Sister.* Eng. trans., New York, 1959.

Photo Album of St Thèrèse of Lisieux. Eng. trans., New York, 1962.

J. Norbury. *St Teresa of Lisieux.* London, 1966.

H. N. Loose. *Thérèse and Lisieux.* Eng. trans., Dublin, 1996.

C. de Meester. *With Empty Hands.* Eng. trans., Tunbridge Wells, 1976.

C. BY ST THERESE, in French

St Thérèse de l'Enfant-Jésus et de la Sainte-Face. Oeuvres complètes. New centenary ed. in 8 vols.. Paris, 1992. An abridged version in one vol. is also available.

Histoire d'une Ame. 1898. Original publication of the version prepared by Mère Agnes.

Lettres de sainte Thérèse de l'Enfant-Jésus. 1948.

Poésies, Textes. Ed. J. Longchamp, Preface by J. Guitton. Paris, 1979.

D. ON ST THERESE, in French

M. Brillant, ill. M. Denis and Mlle Fauré. *La bienheureuse Thérèse de l'Enfant-Jésus: Cantilène pour une jeune sainte.* Paris, 1923.

A. Combes. *Introduction à la spiritualité de Sainte Thérèse de l'Enfant-Jésus.* Paris, 1946.

M. Van Der Meersch. *La petite Sainte Thérèse.* Paris, 1947.

S.-J. Piat. *Histoire d'une famille.* Lisieux, 1947.

C. de Meester. *Dynamique de la confiance.* Paris, 1969.

J.-F. Six. *La véritable enfance de Thérèse de Lisieux—Nevrose et sainteté.* Paris, 1972.

——. *Thérèse de Lisieux au Carmel.* Paris, 1973.

——, and H. N. Loose. *Vie de Thérèse de Lisieux.* Paris, 1975.

——. *Thérèse de Lisieux.* Paris, 1975.

P. Descouvemont. *Sur la terre comme au ciel.* Paris, 1979.

M. More. *La foudre de Dieu.* Paris, 1979.

R. Massol, *Vers la sainteté avec Sainte Thérèse de l'Enfant-Jésus.* Montpellier, 1981.

P. Serant. *L'aventure spirituelle des Normands.* Paris, 1981.

G. Gaucher, R. Pernoud and G. Bailac. *Jeanne et Thérèse.* Paris, 1984.

V. Sion. *Chemin de prière avec Thérèse de Lisieux.* Paris, 1993.

E. Renault. *L'épreuve de la foi.* Paris, 1994.

V. Sion. *Réalisme spirituelle de Thérèse de Lisieux.* Paris, 1994.

G. Gaucher and P. Descouvemont. *Sainte Thérèse de Lisieux.* Paris, 1996.

G.Gaucher. *Jean et Thérèse: Flammes d'amour.* Paris, 1996.

C. de Meester. *Les mains vides—Le message de Thérèse de Lisieux.* Rev. ed., Paris, 1996.

J. Chalon. *Thérèse de Lisieux, une vie d'amour.* Paris, 1996.

P. Descouvemont and H. N. Loose. *Sainte Thérèse de Lisieux: La Vie en images.* Lisieux, 1996.

B. Arminjon. *Thérèse et l'au-delà.* Paris, 1996.

Index of Names